People are asking why America seems to be in decline. The sad fact is we are in a death spiral and it is being done intentionally by liberal far left radicals in the Democrat Party. As Americans, we don't accept responsibility for our actions and in many cases, our inaction. We have grown fat and lethargic, sitting back on our laurels expecting everyone else to work and provide for us.

We have unwittingly transferred our parental responsibilities to the state who intentionally indoctrinate our children in socialist thought through the mass media and public education system. We have created an entire generation of moochers seeking entitlements and free hand outs from the state. Historically and currently, we have elected corrupt politicians who have robbed from the collective treasury and purchased votes through the implementation of socialist designed programs.

Unfortunately, there are far more grasshoppers than there are ants now in the nanny state of America. It is our own fault. There is no one else to blame and we are not victims. We let a fox in the hen house and it has wreaked havoc. We are also responsible to fix what we have broken.

Bill O'Reilly, Fox News analyst and author, was recently questioning ex-Senator Scott Brown of Massachusetts about this very subject. Bill asked the senator how a state of six million educated people can elect politicians and re-elect politicians who have racked up a 60 billion dollar debt in their state. The operative word here is educated. The senator had no answer. I have the answer for Bill.

Yes, the people are educated but what were they taught? What was the social curriculum which trumped math, science and civics? The curriculums we all thought were sacrosanct and being taught in our public schools and colleges. The public schools in Massachusetts and the rest of liberal America have been teaching social justice as perceived by socialists. The children of Massachusetts were taught lessons in diversity. They were taught community service, equality, fairness and the rights to unearned benefits through wealth redistribution. They were taught that capitalism is bad and the rich are the reason for all their problems. Short and simple, they were effectively entrenched in socialist theory and effectively put it into practice in Massachusetts. That is the true answer Bill was looking for in his quest. The citizens of Massachusetts have been completely educated in socialist doctrine indeed.

This book is an analysis and opinion of where America has gone wrong and who is responsible. I hope to encourage those who read this book to join me in my uphill battle to save America from the evils of socialism and the ultimate demise, state tyranny. It is a look into black and white situations that have been masked and mottled into shades of gray. It is a conservative review of America that you will never hear being discussed on your favorite liberal news cast or the publicly tax funded propaganda channels.

America is my country. America is my home and family. America is the greatest nation the world has ever known. She is stumbling but together and with God's help, we will not let her fall.

INTRODUCTION

America is the greatest country in the world. Many conservatives have had their ideas turned around and demonized by a corrupted two party system and an all too complicit and politically biased liberal media. The conservatives represented by the Tea Party, the Patriot Party, the 9/12 project, the Churches, the Libertarian Party and Republican party have been directly attacked by President, Barack Hussein Obama, and his party; the Democrat Party.

It is this party in our two party system, which has been commandeered by a group of bottom dwelling degenerates who have floated to the top of their party and taken control. A collection of far left socialist's zealots, who claim to be liberal progressives. They exist in the establishment of the Republican Party too, but yield little power or influence over the party's majority conservative base. The only "progress" either party can rightfully claim is the progressive destruction of America.

The liberally biased press has openly and intentionally misinformed the American people for quite some time. They have been so derelict in their duties to report information that might expose the lies and corruption in the Obama administration, that our country could rightly be accused of having a state run media not unlike those of communist Russia, China or even North Korea!

I understand the power, greed and corruption inherent in politics even if I find it repulsive. I can even understand why the progressives feel vindicated of white quilt as they parade their affirmative action success before the citizenry like the winning steer at the 4H competition. This is done despite his obvious ineptitude for handling the responsibilities of his high office. However, it is very disheartening to have the press, the guardians of our

Republic, fail the majority of those it has been empowered by the U.S. Constitution to protect.

I like so many of my countrymen and women, have lost faith in the American press and the mainstream media in general. The far left have always dominated the entertainment industry, and that is what the public has grown to expect from the gutters of Hollywood. But the public also has expectations regarding the press. The professional journalists and news reporters, both liberal and conservative, should report the news and not taint the content to anyone's bias. This is not the situation that we find ourselves in today.

The press is supposed to be the standard bearer of blind truth and justice in America. A constitutional power of freedom was bestowed upon the press in the United States like no other organization in the world. Unfortunately, the press has been tainted by those on whom they were to report and the American people pay the price. They knowingly and willingly spread the lies for these despicable politicians and the special interest groups that surround them.

Historically, Americans believed we could rely on journalists to report the facts of a story with an eye for getting at the truth. "Facts are hard evidence" which were checked and rechecked by reporters and editors in their quest to bring truth to the public they served. They were our last line of defense against corruption and tyranny at the highest levels of both business and government. Today, we see a very different enterprise at work.

Many network news personalities and newspaper reporters openly endorse specific politicians and liberal political platforms. Their propensity for selective reporting effectively muzzles dissent and promotes a wholly un-American political agenda to an unwitting and often ignorant public. The truth has taken a back seat to Nielson ratings and ethics/values have been sacrificed for profits. It is no wonder that the press has loss the trust of the American people.

President Obama is the quintessential narcissistic left wing liberal who has no problem implementing unpopular socialist programs in the name of "social justice". He looks condescendingly upon us and acts as if he knows what is best for America; relentlessly pushing his socialist agenda even if it means circumventing the Constitution and Congress to do it. His favorite tool to abuse is the Executive Order which he wields with impunity. One would be hard pressed to find a more dictatorial approach to governance, yet most Americans hardly even notice.

He is often smug and impudent when challenged. He unabashedly abuses the privileges of his office, sitting in the lap of luxury, exempting himself from the healthcare laws he implements, hobnobbing with Sports and Hollywood celebrities while enjoying numerous extravagant taxpayer funded vacations with his family. These trips are funded by _his_ 17 trillion dollar debt which is being placed squarely on the back of our children and grandchildren. It is truly mind boggling how the press and his adoring public can turn a blind eye to his profligacy during one of the worst economic depressions our country has ever had to endure.

The American press can be likened to court jesters and the Democrat Party, a Napoleonic high court of whores who looks down their noses at the rest of us peasants with contempt and derision. President Barak Obama is the perfect example of a contemporary western European elitist aristocrat. It is important to note that the Democrat Party, this President, and the unions to whom they cater are not progressives but are regressives.

This corrupted party and this administration are intent on dismantling the great America that we and generations of Americans before us poured out our blood, sweat and tears to build. They are determined to destroy traditional America and replace it with a Western European/Marxist model state. The Democrat Party has been commandeered by the most radical elements in our society which are being manipulated to legitimize the platform of socialism.

A platform that portends equality but in reality creates an elite ruling class that governs and controls the poor indigent masses using every means available from euthanasia and population management (eugenics /abortion) to surveillance modalities that erode our civil liberties into unrecognizable drivel. They would replace the "American dream" with a "new world order" where only THEY can decide who lives and dies. Hitler had the same idea. Is that the America you want for your children? It will become a reality sooner than you think if you don't actively take a stand to stop it. The decision is yours.

The seeds of communism and socialism grew from the discontent of Karl Marx, Friedrich Engels and Vladimir Lenin, but it has firmly taken root again in the Democrat party. It is a fact that communist sympathizers and spies were prevalent in government during the FDR administration. Now is the time when all the entertainment industry and socialist press will start screaming that McCarthyism was a scam and that there were no communist and that is was just a government witch hunt. I am sorry, but all the denials will not make it less true. There were and still are communists in the federal government, other countries and world organizations which our government funds with our tax dollars.

The so-called party of the people uses public discontent to divide and conquer the American people. They promise to fill our bellies with free food, "entitlements", "Obama

Healthcare", "welfare" call it what you like, but the result is the same. The result is a nanny state that enslaves the populace by creating total dependency on the state. The nanny state that rapes and destroys the middle class until the middle class no longer exists. The void will be filled with an elite class of filthy rich and masses of uneducated dirt poor inner city plantation dwellers with nothing in the middle.

The socialist and communist motto is "from each according to his ability; to each according to his need". It should be obvious that rewarding need by fulfilling that need only creates more need and dependence. This, of course, is antithetical to the independent spirit of most Americans. So how did we get here?

President Obama's re-election was by a slim majority and both of his campaigns were divisive. The Democrat party published and promoted propaganda through the media which was full of lies and false promises. This president proactively attacked and attempted to trivialize the core beliefs of the conservative base because conservatives believe in individual freedom, personal responsibility and personal independence from government tyranny. They seek independence from government interference and seek economic self reliance. This independence, this individualism, is unacceptable thought for a tyrannical state government. You must conform.

The President is laying the foundation for a western European socialist state to be in place by the end of his last term. He is ashamed of America's standing in the world as a superpower which he made clear in his first term. Due to the influence of his Kenyan father, he sees America and its western allies as colonial imperialists who rape the resources from weaker third world nations without adequate compensation. In other words, we don't redistribute enough of our wealth. Colonial powers have oppressed those they conquer. It is a warped view usually shared in elite socialist circles here and abroad both in government and academia.

Obama is indifferent to the fact that we have been spreading democracy around the world so that people can be free to self-rule. He doesn't acknowledge that we have enriched these nations both socially and economically with tons of American taxpayer redistributed wealth (which isn't Constitutional). In the eyes of Obama and the progressives, America and the West must make up for its worldwide aggression and insatiable consumption of resources. This is the reason this President always appoints sympaticos of shame who believe in his warped visions such as Hilary Clinton, Susan Rice, Chuck Hagel and John Kerry.

The legacy of the socialist and communist parties is the total subjugation and dependence of the masses to state tyranny. President Obama and his puppet masters are proponents of government interference and regulation, entitlement programs and wealth redistribution by excessive spending and taxes as a means to this end. Total government dependence can only be achieved through the redistribution of wealth and destruction of the capitalist system. As mentioned previously, Obama's father was a radical communist who believed that colonialist powers needed to be eradicated. His step-father was an Indonesian of the same ilk. It would appear that the proverbial "apple" hasn't fallen far from the tree; worms and all.

The Presidents apparent disregard for the US Constitution with the backing of an SS styled Department of Justice and an activist Judiciary similar to the theocrats ruling Iran is a bold slap in the face of America. The IRS is his political police force hunting down and harassing political opponents. His Department of Homeland Security, his personal national police force, is securing and storing billions of rounds of ammunitions which could only be used on and to control the American people. This is the same Department that has basically stopped deporting illegal aliens that are in our country illegally and threatening our sovereignty. His National Security Agency is spying on all American citizens by collecting every type of electronic data we transmit. What is the next method he will use to circumvent the individual rights of the American people?

The Constitution is seen by this President as an obstacle to get around instead of rules of sound governance and law that should be adhered to, revered and embraced. This is the document America was founded upon. It represents who we are as a people, as a country and his wholesale contempt for its principles and core values are not acceptable!

We should demand that our politicians stay bound to the US Constitution and that they abide by the rule of law. They should be held responsible for enforcing the law too. This should be the minimum requirement for any elected official.

Conservatives have nothing to be ashamed of. We need to remain ethical, moral, proactive, and stand by our convictions. Our message needs to be clear and we need to find alternative methods to get our message out bypassing the liberal media and all those who stand in our way. Obama's water carriers in the media circulate the talking points and propaganda for this administration and actively attack anyone who stands against his federally imposed tyranny.

This book is an attempt to kick-start the discussion. I do not plan on being politically correct or feel that I need to compromise my conservative principles. The liberals never fulfill their end of a deal when they compromise, so why should conservatives be guilted into following through on their end of a deal? We do not need to be deceived and hood winked into a compromise. Is the fence built? Has the flow of illegal immigrants been stopped or has the illegal flood across our borders decreased? Has anything the federal government ever done comprehensively been even remotely successful? Has this administration and the Democrat Party succeeded in destroying our economy by deficit spending thereby eliminating jobs for Americans here at home? We know the answer to that last question positively. YES!

We need to take back America before these degenerates become successful in their attempt to dismantle the greatest country the world has ever known. We need to peacefully protest and get out the vote in order to purge the pestilence in our nation's capitol. We do need to hold elected officials feet to the fire and demand they do the <u>will</u> of the people.

In starting this conversation I would like to be preemptive and prepare you for the slew of attacks against me by the propaganda machine in this country. The more this message hits home, the more I, and other conservatives, will be attacked, ridiculed, persecuted and defamed. In order to jump start the Democrat party defamation playbook tactics, I am going give you a partial list of derogatory names and labels that will be used against me. Unlike the President, I am not that thin skinned nor as brilliant so I may miss a few epitaphs.

I am a white male. I am a staunch capitalist, I am a victim. I am a racist, I am a bigot, and I am a woman. I am a man. I am transgendered. I am Black. I am Hispanic. I am Oriental. I am Mulatto. I am a Mix breed. I did not have sex with that woman, but I have had sex with that other woman. I had sex with that man, and I am asexual. I had sex with myself. I am a homo sapiens. I am a thespian. I am a member of Tea Party. I am a member of the Republican Party. I am a Libertarian. I am a member of the Catholic Church, and I am a Protestant. I am a Muslim. I am a Mormon. I am a Jew. I am Jehovah Witness, I am non-denominational. I am an atheist. I am not an apologist for what I am going to discuss with you in this book and I stand by the freedoms of speech afforded me in the US Constitution to bring these ideas and discussions to the table.

If I have missed any labels or derogatory names that could be tossed in my direction, I am truly sorry. I am sure there will be ample liberal court jesters sucking hind tit at the ready to hurl new and creative names where I left off. After all, they are the Orwellian smear masters. Now, with that being said, let's have some of those pesky uncomfortable discussions.

We Get What We Deserve!

When our great country, the U.S.A, turns against our
strongest ally,
The only democratic nation in the Middle East,
We get what we deserve!

When we follow a President,
who professes that he is not a Muslim,
But whose actions are those of an Islamic sympathizer,
We get what we deserve!

When we elevate privileges to the
equivalency of Inalienable Rights,
We get what we deserve!

When we treat the U.S. Constitution and the Bill of Rights as
evolving documents,
choosing the position that the right's of a class of people
be given more weight than the right's of the individual,
We get what we deserve!

When we deny one's rights as a U.S. Citizen after they paid
their debts to society,
We get what we deserve!

When we invade their privacy with public registrars and
excessive terms of probation,
We get what we deserve!

When we Mirandize illegal aliens and Islamic terrorists,
We get what we deserve!

When we allow anyone to murder and mutilate the unborn
under the guise of a "mother's right" to her body,
or as a convenience to correct a "mistake" as stated by
President Obama,
We get what we deserve!

When we use abortion as gender specific approved murder
under the guise of a cheap form of contraception
We get what we deserve!

When we use abortion as a form of Eugenics
We get what we deserve!

When we don't make consenting adults responsible for their
actions and protect the right to life of the unborn person.
We get what we deserve!

When abortion is not used solely for the protection of the
women's health, or against the crimes of incest and rape as
originally presented to
The American people by our elected leaders,
We get what we deserve!

When we allow corrupt politicians and
an inept attorney general to hold
foreign war combatant trials in U.S. civilian courts instead of
military courts,
affording them the <u>sacred rights</u> of the U.S. Constitution
<u>reserved for American citizens</u>,
We get what we deserve!

When we allow Presidents, Department Secretaries and law
enforcement officials to scapegoat and criminalize members
of our armed services and clandestine operations
in order to protect their own asses thereby
deflecting blame away from their incompetence,
We get what we deserve!

When we allow politicians and government employees to
remain in charge of failed agencies, that failed under their
watch such as Fanny Mae and Freddie Mac
We get what we deserve!

When these same politicians rob the people's treasury to
bail out these failed agencies for which they had oversight,
We get what we deserve!

When the 1st Amendment, Freedom of the Press, is
commandeered and corrupted by the
very press it was written to protect.
We get what we deserve!

When journalism (fact)
is the same as editorials (opinion)
and presented as entertainment (fiction).
We get what we deserve!

When journalists deceive or publish misinformation
with the intent of misleading the American people
and we allow it.
We get what we deserve!

When the Executive participates in cronyism,
appoints campaign finance bundlers
to czars and ambassadorships,
pays them with tax payer dollars without being vetted
or confirmed by members of Congress.
We get what we deserve!

When we allow our politicians to transfer their
Constitutional responsibilities and power over the
American people to political hacks, cronies
and other government agencies,
We get what we deserve!

When we allow the Federal Reserve or the US Treasury to
actively participate in the takeover, bailout and
nationalization of private companies
banks, car companies, insurance industries.
We get what we deserve!

When in fact, we allow them to re-regulate those same
industries which failed under their watch
We are just plain stupid and we get what we deserve!

When the President and his political allies attack
or demean any class of law abiding Americans
While surrounding himself with the racists, terrorists,
communists and other dregs of our society
We get what we deserve!

When any <u>elected member</u> of the Executive, Legislative or
Judicial branch of government is allowed to demean,
slander, liable or publically attack any
U.S. citizen or lawful group of American citizens
who peaceably dissent and they are not impeached
or voted out of office by the American people,
We get what we deserve!

When we don't impose term limits on the U.S. Congress and
the US Supreme Court,
We get what we deserve!

When states don't exercise their sovereign rights and
quit being subservient to the Federal Government.
We get what we deserve!

When we don't demand the Federal Government work
within the strict confines of the U.S. Constitution
and Bill of Rights,
We get what we deserve!

When we don't abolish the current U.S. income tax and
replace it with a
Standard Fair Tax based on sales and
<u>payable by all Americans with no exceptions</u>,
We get what we deserve!

When we allow the U.S. legislature to discuss a VAT tax
(national sales tax) in addition to an increase in income
taxes and we don't peacefully revolt,
We get what we deserve!

When we don't stop the current Administration from
bowing and groveling to foreign world leaders and
selling-out our national sovereignty and our independence.
We get what we deserve!

When we don't stop this Administration and Congress from
stealing our hard earned incomes and then redistributing
our wealth, treasures and assets to the rest of the world,
through the UN, the World Bank
and the International Monetary Fund,
We get what we deserve!

When we don't stop this President and the Congress
from stealing our hard earned incomes and
redistributing our wealth to the degenerates and moochers
in America instead of the truly poor,
We get what we deserve!

When We the People don't abolish the use of tyrannical
executive orders by the President of the United States
even if we need to amend the US Constitution,
We get what we deserve!

When we don't take our country back
from the degenerate politicians,
progressive socialists, communists and the labor unions,
We get what we deserve!

If we don't end the entitlement mentality of having the
government take care of our every need and return to the
individual values; ethics of personal responsibility
and self reliance,
We get what we deserve!

When we demand the Federal government works
within the limits imposed on it by
the US Constitution and the Bill of Rights,
When we return to God,
When we take back our country from a corrupted
and immoral government,
**Then and only then, will we get what we truly deserve!**

On the Precipice of Obscurity!

How the Democrat Party is Destroying America!

Forward

Introduction

We Get What We Deserve!

3) Education
    a) Dummying Down of America – Who teaches the Teachers?
    b) Primary and Secondary Education
    c) Unions Negative Influence on Education
    d) The Best Electorate is an Ignorant Electorate for the Socialist Progressive Democrats

4) Abortion
    a) The Age of Reason
    b) The Losing Arguments for Abortion
    c) Eugenics in Practice
    d) Legalized Murder Should Be Abolished

5) The Reconstruction of the Extended American Family
    a) American Men and Fathers
    b) American Women and Mothers
    c) American Children
    d) The Reconstruction of the Extended Family-Conclusion

More Yet to Come!

Race Relations

Slavery is Over in America and Its Time to move on!

The American Black population and the Democrat/Socialist/ Liberal Progressive Party needs to understand that slavery is over and it is time to move on. One reason that race is still an issue in the United States is because there are liberal progressives in both parties who benefit themselves by keeping the contentious and vitriolic atmosphere alive for their own political and financial gain. Don't fool yourselves into thinking that the majority of Americans approves of slavery or questions the equality of the black race in American society today. We don't.

If anything, the divisive programs promoted by the Democrat Party, such as affirmative action, reverse discrimination and racially based quota systems are slapping most white Americans in the face. Many of these issues have nothing to do with slavery only the proliferation of ignorance and prejudice to get the black vote through the perpetual indoctrination in victimhood.

Yes, of course there are still prejudices born out of ignorance on all sides of the racial spectrum. The New Black Panther is no different than an Aryan white supremist. Many prejudices are simply because there are a lot of ignorant people out there.

But there are far more situations that exist that are designed and implemented to serve a political purpose. The politicians play on the anger of the blacks in the black districts or the anger of the whites in the white districts. Who was it said "never waste a good crisis" or something along those lines. I believe it was a political hack from Chicago who just happens to be a liberal progressive Democrat. Remember too that it is the Democrats who intentionally create the crisis from which to exploit.

If you control the basics of food, water, clothing, health and education, you control the masses. This is the Progressive liberal mantra. It is much easier to mislead an ignorant and brainwashed mass of people than to mislead one independent intelligent person.

However, today's prejudice that most white American's experience is not about the black race being black. It is not the myth of black's intellectual inferiority, regret over the loss of slavery or the subjugation of the whites in the South by the North during Reconstruction. There was a time when that was applicable, but this is not that time.

The majority of whites have "evolved" beyond that time. In all honesty, I think blacks are as responsible and as guilty as whites of being racists; if not more so than whites. The only difference between the two is that American blacks are encouraged to harbor their animosity and expected to use the victim or race cards for whatever plight they suffer at any given time. They are also taught to remember it is always the white man's fault no matter what befalls them. They are always expected to be the perpetual victim. This victim behavior is heavily promoted by the liberal political class and their puppets in the media.

Prejudice today is caused by the implementation of government entitlement programs that cater to one class, gender or race of people on the backs of another class, gender or race. It is further aggravated by affirmative action, reverse discrimination and quotas. These programs are mandated by the federal, state and local governments.

These programs are implemented and reinforced through the public education system. This "divide and conquer "strategy is a political tool used to get votes, attain power, greed and to skim money from the public purse. In reality, politicians intentionally lower standards for success and achievement through public education and other socially engineered programs.

This indoctrination is imposed on all Americans regardless of race. We'll address some of today's problems with public education or institutional indoctrination further down the road in greater detail. Hopefully through a series of books, we will be able to tackle many of the problems destroying and infecting the very core of American exceptionalism. But the slavery of the past should not be confused with the slavery of today in America.

The tension between the races and in many cases gender, have been further aggravated by affirmative action and the constant exploitation of its use by the national media and the political class. Both the media and the political class expect whites to hang their heads and walk on their knees pounding their breasts for their fore fathers transgressions. There is this nagging perception that whites need to continually beg for forgiveness for all the bad things that have happened to black Americans in the past.

Those days should be long gone. Of course, they are not gone at all, which is why we are having these pointed discussions. I do not feel one bit of anxiety nor regret over a past that I had no part in or control over. That would be equivalent to me feeling responsible for forcing American Indians onto the reservations (where they remain to this day), or the death of the Jews in the Holocausts. It's history. It's unfortunate. It happened. It's over. Learn from it and don't repeat it. Move on!

If we are to learn anything from the Indian experience or slavery it is how completely incompetent the federal government is at handling anything "comprehensively." Other than military excellence and success of our armed forces, I can't think of or find one federal program that has been a success for America. Even our great military apparatus is subject to procurement and contracting fraud as well as political manipulation inside the Washington DC beltway. The way things are being politically manipulated by this administration and Congress even our one great success seems to be at risk. Our national sovereignty is being tossed around like a ping pong ball by a bunch of political whores.

They parade FDR around like they parade President Obama as a success of the Progressive Movement. News Flash! FDR didn't save the country from the Great Depression and Obama is not an affirmative action success story. Capitalism and Industrialism saved America. It will be again after we eliminate the progressives in government.

FDR was an isolationist who avoided war and was on the verge of destroying the United States economically until he was reluctantly forced into the war by the attack on Pearl Harbor. Much like Obama disrespects Israel, our staunch Middle East ally, FDR's isolationist approach showed disrespect to our allies. He would not commit to war for more than two years after the start or WWII until his hand was forced. FDR was deficit spending our nation into a financial abyss and selling out our national sovereignty at the same time! It would seem there are many negative parallels between the two "Democrat Progressive" administrations.

The American people with an economy based on capitalism and industrial innovation won the war. Franklin D. Roosevelt was a progressive liberal disaster who encouraged the tenets of socialism. He raided the US Treasury and started a number of entitlement programs as his solution to the Great Depression. We are still paying for those disasters today. After President Woodrow Wilson, Franklin D. Roosevelt should be remembered as the Father of American Socialism and Barack Obama his son.

Social Security is not an entitlement program, so that discussion is moot. Americans paid their work dollars into this system that the federal government pillaged and mismanaged. It is still a mismanaged bankrupt example of federal ineptitude. Social Security's insolvency in government control should speak volumes about government's inability to manage anything. But let's get back to our discussion of slavery.

Historically, Southerners did not start out harboring animosity towards blacks. They were an owned possession, an asset, and provided valuable services to the Southern states. Many in the North, and by no means the majority, did find slavery to be abhorrent but many owned slaves themselves. This is not a justification for slavery, just a note on hypocrisy (another tool of the Democrat Party).

The first slaves came to America during the years when America was a group of fractious colonies in the 1600's. There were slaves on the Spanish galleons that conquered and traded throughout the Caribbean and South American prior to the establishment of the colonies. Since the inception of the monarch systems in Europe, there was indentured servitude.

Early Egypt had slaves and most conquered people in biblical times became slaves to their conquerors. Slavery was not uniquely an American operation, though some would make you believe this to be the case. Slavery was imported and smuggled into America much like the current day illegal aliens. America is but a pup on the pages of slavery. Yet, her wounds are constantly salted and never allowed to heal.

During the Continental Congress, the founding fathers of the U.S. were trying to unify a fractious group of colonies with conflicting governmental charters, religions and moral positions. There were adamant objections to slavery by the Quakers of Pennsylvania as well as other religious and social groups. Like today's radicals-NOW, Green Peace, PETA the Old and New Black Panthers, the Muslim Brotherhood, the Democrats and numerous other fringe groups, the abolitionists protested and spread propaganda to suit their purposes.

They did have ethical and moral religious doctrine against slavery which today would be viewed as an argument between the separation of church and state clause. However, we were still not a unified country under the Constitution, nor the amendments which freed the slaves, so there is no need to have that laborious discussion.

The Northern and Southern colonies, and later the States, continued to volley the slavery issue for more than 100 years. Each compromise left the slavery issue sitting on a political fence, up to and until the Civil War. The war ended the immoral practice of slavery but at huge costs of American blood and treasure. The war destroyed the economies of the North and the South which were intricately dependent on one another prior to the war.

In losing the Civil War and then during the Reconstruction period after the war, blacks became the scorn of the Southern plight. In essence, the child was spanked by the parent, and the child kicked the dog.

Yes, in many cases, and through no fault of their own, the freed slaves bore the brunt of the South's anger and resentment. In actuality, the North should have borne the brunt of the South's anger and resentment. After all it was the fault of the Yankees for interfering in the business of the South. It was a business issue at the time in the South, not necessarily a moral issue. Remember that slaves were not considered people, but possessions. Therefore, Southerners didn't see slavery as a humanly moral issue but one of economic scale.

"To the victors go the spoils," as the saying goes. Even though Abraham Lincoln wanted the reunion of the states to be peaceful and all Americans to be reunited under the flag expeditiously, his assassination didn't let his desires come to fruition. The anger against the southern blacks constantly manifested itself in a growing resentment and hatred shown by southern whites during and then for a long time after the Civil War.

This same contempt was inflicted on all remaining free blacks whom made their exodus to the North by the northern whites too. This resentment and contempt for the freed slaves was shared by both whites in the North and the South, but for different reasons.

The South was an agrarian society, totally dependent on slave labor. The importance of slave labor to the success of the plantation was indisputable. The Southern States and their plantation owners had considerable wealth and a vibrant economy prior to the Civil War. The South's agricultural base was devastated by the loss of slavery. The machines necessary to replace this manual labor hadn't been invented yet. So the loss of labor was catastrophic to the plantation system. Needless to say, abolition of slavery was a major blow to the economies of the South since slavery was so intricately tied to agriculture and production.

The South provided agricultural products, both finished and unfinished, to the North and to Europe. Unfinished products such as cotton and high grade minerals such as iron ore where shipped North and abroad as was sugar, vegetables, potatoes, rice and other food stuffs. These items were essential to feeding the booming northern populations. It was the South's economic bread and butter

The North had a booming industrial economy prior to the Civil War and was dependent on the raw materials from the South for their manufacturing base. This loss of slavery had a devastating effect on the whole Southern economy, and as a result it had a substantially negative effect on the Northern economy as well.

The southerners defeat in the Civil War, the degradation and subjugation inflicted by the North on the South during Reconstruction, found the wrath of the Southern whites and their fury inflicted on the newly freed slaves. This angst also befell the carpetbagger Yankees who then invaded the South.

During the war and at the end of the war, a mass exodus of black men, women and children moved to the North where a new hell awaited them. Though a small segment of the northern population were staunch abolitionists, the new influx of black people created a severe burden on the urban infrastructures in the North.

There were white job shortages due to all the men returning from the war. There were other ethnic and cultural divides to cross. There was a continuing influx of European immigrants streaming into the country which were further straining a delicate infrastructure. There was insufficient housing, schools and sanitation. Social services, churches and charities were working as hard as they could to provide assistance to the poor, orphans and homeless.

Soon enough the politicians in the North and South would have a new ripe group of victims to whom they would pander. This new class was the black American. In haste to accommodate the new mass of refugees, the inner city plantation was created. The Democrat Party had a new class to nurture and indoctrinate into victimhood.

American Blacks do not Assimilate
because Other Americans Accommodate

 Many of the Negroes fleeing from the South after the Civil
War were neither educated nor trained in a trade other than
agriculture, and therefore could not provide skilled labor. If
per chance they were skilled, they were relegated to second
behind their white brothers.

The majority could not read nor write. In reality, this
ignorance added to their burden because the lack of
education and job skills limited the Negroes ability to rise
out of poverty. This was a real tragedy which was a direct
result of slavery and further advanced through the spoils of
war. The lack of a good public education has continued the
plight of the black man and the poor to the current day.

It was easy for the new European immigrants to demean the
new poor kid on the block. They were poorer and less
educated than themselves. It was ok that you were a freed
slave as long as "you and your kind stayed in your place."
This was no longer a North or South issue. It was the freed
black's station in American life, period. It ultimately led to
the creation of the inner city plantation, the poorest
neighborhoods in urban America.

Progressive liberals do not like this term; inner city
plantation. It is a slant exposing their failed programs. Or is
it in fact, exactly what it is by their intentional design?
Sometimes the truth can hurt when exposed to the light and
become quite uncomfortable.

There was existing ethnic strife in the large cities from the diversity of European immigrants whom sought refuge in America. Some came because of famine; others came to escape religious or political persecution. Although the immigrants assimilated into the American culture, they held strongly to their traditions and the ways of their native countries.

I think the American melting pot metaphor is incorrect. I think an American Stew Pot is more appropriate. Here everyone assimilates into the American culture but adds his own unique texture and flavor to the pot; together but separate.

Because the blacks were brought to America against their will as slaves, they felt and many still feel that they did not and do not belong here. Yes, they were shunned by white society before and after the Civil War by both Americans and European immigrants. When you don't belong, then you don't feel the need or the desire to assimilate. However, that was then and this is now. We all need to assimilate into America.

Many blacks refuse to assimilate into American culture and many politicians, elitist and educators accommodate, advocate and appease these positions. As previously stated, they all gain in one way or another at the expense of the black American's position.

Of course, when you don't assimilate you become alienated and ostracized. American Blacks were the odd man out and in many cases still are. Negroes in America are in fact treated with prejudice. If one doesn't make an effort to fit in, he won't fit in. You become a self-imposed *victim.* There is nothing a politician likes more than a *victim* that needs their help; a politician who can truly feel your pain.

Black Americans are not special because of the past slavery. They are not special because they are of African descent. Black Americans are special because they are American; an important part of American culture. They aren't a part of slavery even if they have ancestors that were slaves. One is not a Nazi just because one is a German.

White Americans today aren't responsible for the slavery of the past or subjects to a King. (Although this President does at times appear to be more of a monarchy than the leader of a democratic republic.) We are not responsible for the sins of our fathers. It is however a historical fact that Black's are in America as a consequence of slavery.

But more importantly, blacks are an intricate part of American society. You are in the greatest democratic republic the world has ever known. By not assimilating into the American fabric, blacks are destroying the very fabric that makes this country great. Blacks are passing on their opportunity to reach their full potential. American Blacks are not in a socialist country were individuality and success are scorned. They are in America.

For the black race, the black culture and for the advancement of American goals, black assimilation needs to occur. Christians don't get reparations from Rome for atrocities in the Coliseum. We don't even have to talk about the Holocaust or the lack of reparations for the Indians or Japanese.

This festering wound of the past has not been allowed to heal so assimilation and inclusion can take place. But black Americans are indeed suffering as a result of this maternal accommodation mentality. Those whom reparations would have been due are now dead and gone. Those responsible for the sins of the past are long gone too. The new sin, the real sin, is practiced by those who keep black Americans in the bondage of ignorance and political servitude.

As part of the Mea Culpa regime, white Americans have been forced to give blacks a pass that no other race in America has been given. Blacks are not required to assimilate into American society like all other cultures; all to America's detriment.

While discrimination against blacks is abhorrent, reverse discrimination against whites is completely acceptable to the far left liberals. This too is an American travesty of justice. It should be just as abhorrent for any American to be discriminated against.

You can't blame whites for being a little resentful unless you are in the liberal media or a mealy mouth pandering politician with a vote to gain. It is in the best interest of the politicians, media and the educational institutions to keep blacks from assimilating. They all grow more powerful and profit financially from the division and chaos. It is to their benefit to keep American blacks on the plantation.

In fact, blacks in America are rewarded for not assimilating. They are rewarded for not achieving. A majority of blacks are huddled into inner city plantations, where they are contained and paraded to the public-at-large by the mainstream media as abused, oppressed, poor and uneducated. Isn't this blatant prejudice? All the things which politicians and the social progressives promise over and over again to eliminate if you vote for them.

Every anchor on the evening news is looking for an inner city sob story. They get more viewers and more ratings by pulling on the heart strings of a caring American public.

Politicians run with those stories with a promise to fix the problems by throwing gobs of money at the problem to secure votes. Of course, it's not their money and the problems are never fixed regardless of the amount of money thrown. The monies never reach the poor but line the pockets of the bureaucrats down the political chain; round and round we all go.

Then more piles of money are thrown to the public school systems for affirmative action, social promotion, school meal programs, aftercare, childcare and other socialist training programs...like one of my all time favorites, "um um Obama." These are the very same politicians who promise to eradicate problems but never succeed and only make matters worse. How foolish of you to think that this separation of race by our leaders would lead to racial discontent or prejudice!

The current position of blacks in America and the unintended result of most government social programs (assuming they are unintended-nah!) is indisputable proof that everything the federal government tries to do fails miserably. There is one exception and the only one provided for in the U.S. Constitution-the protection of the nation by our armed forces. Even our armed services can't escape the corruption of the politicians responsible for their funding. Of course, you need to understand that our armed forces, our only true semblance of a government success, are considered a failure by the liberal Progressives.

You have to look no further than Welfare, Medicare, Medicaid, Public Education, Food Stamps, and Social Security to experience the magnitude of a massive government and its massive "comprehensive" failures.

The sad part is that many blacks and many poor are missing the opportunities afforded by the private sector and capitalism in America. This is because many blacks are chained to the shackles of poverty and stumbling under the yoke of perpetual ignorance fostered through our public school systems secured in their place by government. This bondage is for the good of the elected officials, the political elites who care nothing about one station in life. They are no longer part-time political servants. They are life time political elite parasites going from one campaign to another.

The black community needs to wake up and realize it is not the whites that are holding them down; it is the government and other appendages of the public sector. There are plenty of black Americans in government actively holding their brothers down too! A prime example would be the Black caucus in Congress.

The new "en Vogue" oppression is politically based and beneficial only to the oppressors. Oppression was forced during the slave trade and prior to the Civil War here in America. It is currently practiced in other areas of the world in its original state. Not always against race, but against tribe, against a nationality, a gender and religion as well. But it is not a real forced oppression now in America. It is a masked oppression of servitude to government and the state. You have relinquished your freedom to the state. Once you relinquish a right as precious as your freedom to the government, it is virtually impossible to get it back. That is the real travesty behind the Patriot Act. What we gave up we shall never get back and it was priceless.

Blacks are not owned as chattel, they are owned for their vote. They are owned so that they will be indebted and need the government. They drain valuable tax dollars out of an already strained and inefficient welfare system. It is an oppression born of the pity-pot moocher entitlement class that gets past down from government-parent to government- child. As a professor once told me, "Waldo's beget Waldo's."

It is the political programs designed to promote failure and dependency on the state instead of individual success. It is further engrained in the poor of our society by failing public school systems. Again, these education systems are implemented to guarantee failure. The politicians use the liberal media outlets to encourage plight and dependence. These are all degenerative systems instituted by the liberal/progressive/socialists/communist/fascist in our government. Systems put in place by the party of the people, the Democrat party which operates within our federal, state, and local governments. It is not in their best interests to lose control of their constituency. Control is power.

Intelligence and independence trumps skin color and this is what makes America exceptional. It is not in the politician's best interest for the blacks in America to assimilate. It is not in the politician's best interest for blacks to be educated. If they assimilate and embrace the freedoms afforded them in America, they would be independent of the controls of government. They would feel empowered instead of entitled. "Progressives" can't have that. They have to keep all Americans black, Latin, Asian, white, men and women, ignorant, divided, subjugated and enslaved for the state to stay in power and maintain total control; to work their will on the people.

These degenerates no longer hide in the shadows like Hess and the other communists did during FDR's administration. Like during the Mc McCarthy era, many in the entertainment industry and politics promote socialist ideals as progressive. They have slogans like Bend Over, Lean Forward, or Grab Your Knees. They are showing their colors in broad daylight and at the expense of those whom they entertain or serve.

Liberals are represented by private and public union thugs. They are represented by far-left lobbyists, political action committees, think tanks, pollsters, foundations and other special interests groups. They operate in the open in America and claim to carry the chalice of America's greatness. In actuality they ensure America's demise. Black poverty and ignorance are the result of the Democrat Socialist Party in America and black poverty and ignorance is necessary for them to remain in power.

I contend very shortly, if it hasn't already happened, that they will secure the fall of our great country unless we take individual responsibility and rise up against them. They surely are not here to help the poor or down trodden and statistics prove they have failed the poor and the black population specifically, completely, and miserably.

The problem with the Progressives is that they steal through taxation from A to give B under the heading of "Free" instead of theft. Of course, the beneficiary is all too eager to accept something that they didn't have to earn. The liberal Progressives call it redistribution of wealth, but in actuality it is blatant theft.

They call lying, misinformation, but it is still outright lies. You work your ass off to get ahead for you and your family, and the government forcibly takes it from you to give it to someone who has not earned it. Not to build a road, sewage system (unless you count Washington, D.C.), or something from which all the public benefits. No. The Regressives need redistribution of wealth to further divide the races and the electorate.

Do you ever notice that those who cry for equality and those who propose redistribution of wealth never practice what they preach? How many of your politicians voluntarily give their millions attained while in office to the IRS? How many pay extra taxes? Why are so many politicians being investigated for tax evasion-white, black, Republican, Democrat?

How can any legal law abiding citizen re-elect a coke head to be Mayor of DC or a Congressman who is under investigation for not paying his fair share of taxes? How could President Obama appoint and Congress confirm a US Treasury Secretary who didn't pay all of his taxes? We all make mistakes and we can forgive someone their mistakes but do you put them back in charge of the candy jar?!! Idiots!

The reason that black people don't assimilate is because it is simply not in their best interests to do so. When you are provided with all your needs to survive, but not succeed, you lose whatever drive you had to succeed and you become complacent and comfortable. Until it becomes necessary to institute austerity measures, then the uncontrollable riots would begin.

After providing the poor with fine digs in the inner city plantation, the next thing the state has to accomplish is to dumb them down and keep them contained and quiet; thus they created government operated public education.

The only problem with this concept is that in a democratic republic based on capitalism, education would be privately funded and controlled locally. Private education is far superior to all forms of public education in America. Private education would teach competition, self reliance, self promotion and the benefits of individual exceptionalism. It would teach core academic studies and provide a solid foundation for advancement and employment opportunities. Schools would be operated and funded locally by the people in their own neighborhoods. This system of education would and does present a major road block for socialism.

The federal government has corrected this little socialist roadblock by creating a federal education department run by the nanny state operating in Washington DC controlling the money and curriculums in the local public school systems. The "Nanny State Mother" in Washington D.C. will redistribute stolen taxes to your school on your behalf for your health, education and welfare provided you obey their rules and mandates. Thus you have the American public school system; provide poor education, check!

They will steal from the workers in the country to feed you. Free food and clothing, check! All of the Progressive problems solved through the social justice concept of wealth redistribution! Now don't you just feel all warm and fuzzy! What does the government do when the providers refuse to pay for the moochers or worse, quit producing? It will happen eventually.

All other cultures that have legally set foot upon America's shores have assimilated into American society except for the African culture. Even the illegal aliens have made a better attempt at assimilation in order to avoid deportation.

In our white guilt we feel the maternal need to coddle, pamper, protect, care for and completely enable the poor black man, woman and child. This enabling has the same affect that enabling an Alcoholic does; the status quo never changes. There is no need to assimilate or meld into a society when you can maintain your autonomy and depend on someone else to take care of all your needs and be responsible for all your problems.

This is why Puerto Rico doesn't become a state but remains a US Commonwealth. They can suck off the US Treasury, maintain their autonomy and get all the benefits without incurring any of the costs associated with being the 51st State. They would be foolish to become a state.

After all, black Americans are a victim of this society and none of this lack of responsibility is their fault. This is what the government and its propaganda media arm tells us to believe. This is exactly what the Progressive movement needs to occur in order to attain their holy grail- _total dependence on the state._

Close the Inner City Plantations

Inner city projects are the most egregious examples of failed government experiments. It doesn't matter if you call them plantations, slums, hoods or even pretty names like Overtown, Harlem or the South Side. They remain failed social experiments; that is unless you think this contemporary form of slavery is acceptable.

I don't think they started out as good intentioned social justice experiments. I think they started as a place to relocate poor Europeans and freed black people when they migrated to the north. A place to keep the poor contained and out of the way. This is most definitely the federal position today.

The North was predominantly white European immigrants and more immigrants were arriving daily. Many Northern men were returning home from the Civil War and were looking to get a job and get their own lives back in order. As time progressed, the blacks were competing for a limited number of skilled and unskilled jobs which caused a lot of social discontent for both blacks and whites.

During Reconstruction and even earlier on, during the Underground Railroad period, the blacks fled from the south to the north. It is important to remember that the blacks were freed but still subject to racism, bias and hatred in the south which was intensified by the recent war. The results of a civil war were the elimination of more than half of the white male population in the North and South. The blacks bore the brunt of that anger and not just from Southerners.

The abolitionists and religious zealots of the time had achieved their goals of freedom for the black slaves but at a horrendous cost to the nation. It was the start of a new race war, where blacks were blamed for the war between the whites. Similar to the historical fall guys of all time, the Jews, the blacks became the scapegoat for the nation's ills. There was no love lost or adoration in either white community, the North or the South, for the black man. The freed African slave was an added burden to a fractured society in the North as well.

However, our recollections of history are often mired in folklore and not fact. The North was more concerned with preserving the Union and jump starting the economy than liberating the black man. The North also wrote the history books that are being taught in our schools. This history may be a little prejudiced and skewed in favor of the victor.

The current day perpetual mantra for slavery remorse has been further aggravated by affirmative action, reverse discrimination, quotas and the constant exploitation of race baiting" by the political class, the Department of Justice and the national media. They hang clinging to the broken chains of the civil rights movement "feeling your pain." We'll discuss these issues later. They collectively keep the wounds open and salted for their own political and financial gain.

As I have said before, I do not personally feel one bit of anxiety nor regret over a past that I had no part in or control over. I have empathy for those victims definitely, but responsibility, absolutely not. I offer no Mea Culpa, nor guilt, nor remorse. I think any wasted conversation on reparations for black Americans or the Japanese Americans during WWII is a joke antagonized by a group of far left idiots stuck in a constant state of cultural penance.

If there weren't reparations when it happened, then those who were liable at the time got away with their crimes. This is true for Bill Clinton and continues to be true for Barry Obama too!

Is it mine or your responsibility to pay for the crimes of another? There are many pulpit puppets and race baiting politicians such as Al Sharpton, Jesse Jackson Sr., Jesse Jr., Bill Clinton, Barack Obama, Rev. Wright, Louis Farrakhan, and many, many other inner-city plantation overseers and masters. They work as community organizers, spiritual leaders and social panderers in local neighborhoods, on state capitol steps and in the halls of Congress. They need the incendiary memory of slavery kept alive to attain political power and fill their pockets with illicit financial gain.

These pulpit pushers and political hacks aren't exactly carrying on the work of Mother Teresa and are a far cry from MLK jr. They canvass the inner city plantation and remind "their kind" of the current oppression and the past transgressions perpetrated by others. They mock and pander to them from the pulpit with fake southern accents like Hillary Clinton or soul slang and swagger from the Big BO trying to collect a vote. The separation of church and state is only applicable to republican or conservative candidates. Only Democrats are given a pass to pander from the pulpit.

You can watch these circus side shows on NBC, CBS, or ABC to name a few of more *trusted* news sources. They are always ready to point a camera and apparently condone any race baiting performed by President Obama, Hillary Clinton or any other Democrat pandering to the black race. You are left to assume that the people being preached to are too ignorant to even see that they are being mocked or the audience could simply be complacent racists who agree with these socialist demagogues.

These faux leaders promote hatred over healing. These snake oil salesmen and saleswomen are hypocrites that financially gain from their fleeced flock. They use their podiums and teleprompters to further incite and divide this nation by class, gender and yes, race.

They never fulfill their empty promises but they insist that they can feel your pain and if elected and re-elected and re-elected they will eventually alleviate that pain. It never happens, never happened and never will!

Sorry, this is not cynicism; this is a sad matter of fact. Each time that we are a party to these failed social policies and programs, we fall further and further as a nation. The more deceit and deception the politicians promote the more poverty they excrete.

There is one thing for certain. The political class always has money available to keep the inner city neighborhoods poor and full. They are full of people, full of crime, full of litter, full of bad public schools, full of bad transportation and those who oversee these destitute neighborhoods and keep the poor being poor are frankly full of shit.

It's trickle down Democrat party policy. Corruption, division and pandering from the President of the United States, down to the state and then down to your local communities. A tax dollar is confiscated and sent to Washington and less than a penny makes it back to the plantation or the truly poor.

By promoting Obama's election and proven failed policies, the poor and blacks specifically, are misled into believing that wealth redistribution would be tolerated by the majority of working Americans. They believe that they, the poor, would benefit substantially from the theft of the US Treasury? They are mistaken.

Black Americans have been indoctrinated into an entitlement mentality. Do blacks Americans think they will get lots of "Obama money?" Are they better off today than four years ago? Are blacks better off then when they first were freed, traveled the Underground Railroad and planted their roots in the cesspools created in the inner cities of America?

Although Obama and the Democrats in Congress have been successful in their theft of over 5 Trillion dollars in four years, have the poor substantially benefitted? I know the unions have benefited. I know teachers, police, firefighters and other political special interests have benefitted handsomely.

I know the Democrats are big on blaming Wall Street while accepting huge campaign contributions through the back door. Like all sleazy politicians they are immoral hypocrites. Why doesn't the press give a listing of Wall Street bundlers that endorsed Obama and now hold positions in his administration?

I am also aware that the federal government, more specifically the Executive Branch (without Constitutional authority) took tax payer money and saddled us with excessive debt to bail out failed public and private financial institutions; institutions deemed too big to fail. The government printed cash out of thin air and gave the money to these financial conglomerates. An enormous and immoral debt placed on the back of yours and my children.

In addition, these titans of industry who received the bailouts and the money printed out of thin air, have no one and no where to invest those ill gotten funds because the economy is in the tank from government regulations, excessive interference and astronomical debt. You won't hear that on your favorite mainstream news channels.

Have black Americans risen out of poverty or have their votes been bought and their station in life <u>as permanently poor</u> been secured by Obama and the ilk that has taken over our federal government? I think the answer to that question is self-evident.

You can divert your attention to Jerry Springer, Judge Judy or the comedy show known as the annual State of the Union Address, but has the station of the poor improved in America? Has the state of the poor fundamentally changed under President and Congress? His policies have been very successful. They have been successful in creating more poor and destitute while destroying what is left of the middle class. So I guess it just depends on what kind of success you were expecting; what fundamental transformation you were looking for in America.

But let's get back to the discussion of inner city plantations. There were more than 2 million slaves in America at the end of the civil war. You have a mass influx of poor people looking for work, a place to live, new locations to set down roots. There are far too many people and even fewer jobs because America was just recovering from a major civil war.

Most white people at the time were taught at home or a local school house that the black race was inferior to the white race. This did not just occur in the rural South. It was prevalent in the mindset of the educated and high society of the North also.

Prejudice was geared toward a race, but not always a hatred of that race. A prejudice based on ignorance. They just needed someone to blame for their own problems and the black man was the right person at the right place at the right time. They are not the first race to be the scapegoat and to take the heat for others actions. The Jews, the Christians and many others have been oppressed for the benefit of others.

It did not take long for inner city slums or the areas I designate as inner city plantations to come into being. There is Harlem, the Southside of Chicago, all of Los Angeles, Overtown Miami, the Ninth Ward and the entire state of California, to name a few. The foundation of these areas is not any different than the working plantation systems they supplanted. New owners, overseers and chains shackling the very people they claim to represent and help.

In the 1950's the white male of the Deep South was the father, breadwinner, husband, and pillar of strength in the American family. In the deep South, the Black male lived on the other side of the tracks, were poorer than his white brother, but he prayed with his Bible, raised his family, and went to work every day. He too was the breadwinner and pillar of strength in his family. He knew there was a better way in America, and taught his family to rise above the fray. He worked hard so his children could get an education.

Yes, there was mutual discrimination, prejudices, racism and inequalities, but there was a strained co-existence. There was however one America in the South. Many injustices were addressed during the Civil Rights era, but prejudices remained in both the white and black communities. If the two races would have assimilated after the Civil War, in the South and the North, a large portion of this book wouldn't need to be written.

I didn't say it was a just or always peaceful co-existence in the South, but it was better than what happened to the majority of American Negroes who migrated to the North. They became and still are pawns of the local, state and federal governments. They are pawns of the Democrat Party.

Prior to the Civil War, the plantation owner was the landowner and economic center. He held the purse strings. He fulfilled every need for the slaves in return for their services; indentured or freed. He ordered them to work in the fields, the home, the gardens and indeed all the grounds of the plantation. Some but not all slaves were provided an education and were instructed in the teachings of the Christian church. African culture and religions were considered primal and barbaric in the South and the North.

The blacks planted, irrigated, fertilized and harvested all the crops in addition to all the other services they provided. Although cotton was king and provided economic security, most plantations were primarily self-sufficient and self sustaining. In the south, many were only small farms with few if any slaves. It would be accurate to say that the black slaves produced every form of farm sustenance. It was a way of life in the southern states of America for the better part of two hundred years and a part of her history; blemishes and all.

After the war, the South was not going to be subservient to both the North and the Negro. During Reconstruction, the North intentionally tried to subjugate the South both financially and legally. The war was over but the reunification battle had just begun and someone was going to pay for this terrible war.

Almost immediately the South was forced to accommodate the Negro and endure this new political animosity imposed on it by the North. The North invaded the south with Yankee Carpetbaggers who laid claim to land and took over southern businesses. The federal government began legislating punitive actions to further retaliate against the South. The federal government did preserve the union of the states, but there were cost incurred and costs to be repaid by the South.

The Southern Democrats retaliated against the blacks with a number of discriminatory laws and forced segregation. They instituted Jim Crow laws, segregated schools and instituted other laws to keep the black man in "his place."The birth of the Klu Klux Klan was a result of this tumultuous period in history.

Blacks and whites lived separate, but not equal lives. That would be much later and cover many more hurdles culminating in the Civil Rights movement. It would eventually come and America would fix her mistakes. It seems evident to me that while we were looking to correct the travesty of slavery, we were recreating the same plantation system in our cities. Or were the political elite just moving the hidden ball under the cups?

It is interesting to study the progression from the southern plantations to the inner city. The Southern Plantation owner profited from the black community. In reality, the plantation owner was utterly dependent on the black labor which provided the produce and materials the plantation owner sold. In return, the Southerners accumulated wealth and became upstanding members of American society while blacks toiled in bondage.

In the Inner City, the position of the plantation owner and slave master is a group of individuals profiting off the poor heirs of past slaves. In the private sector it is the slumlord. In the public domain it is the local, state and federal governments.

The slumlord is one of the slave owners. He profits off the rents either paid for by the black renter, or paid by the local, state, or federal subsidy. These funds are provided through taxation, wealth redistribution for the benefit of the poor. This is government's form of charity or vote purchasing. You choose.

The Local, State, and Federal politicians are the other plantation owners who financially profit and gain political power by getting the poor blacks to vote for them. In return for their votes, the inner city plantation occupants get their entire existence off the theft or "redistribution" from other tax payers.

This helps the politicians achieve their goals through the use of race based tyranny. They use race baiting and race bias, in order to justify stealing from Peter to pay for Paul; all the while skimming a little off the top for themselves along the way. They promote their positions as moral justifications and obligations placed on the state to help the poor.

The Constitution does not recognize or authorize this social engineering which is being provided by government. This is the result of Constitutional interpretation through executive, legislative and judiciary "Evolution." Moreover, this is an imperative socialist tenet required to keep the plantations funded and operational. It is socialist justification for circumventing the Constitution and raiding the US Treasury. This is the methodology of the Democrat Party.

The poor and a disproportionate number of American blacks have been moved into government projects, row houses, surrounded by fences and barbed wire. They fill blocks and blocks of inner city areas with blight and poverty. For all intensive purposes, they are internment and indoctrination camps that regrettably still exist and function at full capacity today.

The only difference between these projects in America and the rest of the slums in the world are that people in American slums have the opportunity to escape the bonds of poverty. These are the individual freedoms guaranteed by the US Constitution, not by a tyrannical administration, Congress, judiciary or state.

Of course, the more government control that is exerted over the individual, the less likely the individual will be able to control his own destiny. This severely limits the poor individual's ability to rise out of poverty. Individualism is not what is taught in inner city public schools and it surely not in the best interest of the socialist class or state.

The unions, police, and the public education system, are the slave masters. They are on the tax payer payroll provided by the plantation owners who are making sure to keep those pesky poor people in their place.

Unions inherently protect the weakest link in their food chain. The worst teachers, worst police officers and the worst public service providers are protected by their union masters. Union bosses and union employees profit from high salaries and fantastic compensation packages. They do nothing to raise the poor up through quality public education because they do not provide it. It is not in their best interest. Their job is to keep the inner city kids ignorant, inner city adults contained while protecting and preserving their member's benefits.

This travesty is being perpetrated on the poor indoctrinating an entire younger generation poor and middle class alike with "free" entitlements such as contraception, such as government funded abortion. God forbid the poor or their children should read, write, become proficient in arithmetic or learns a viable trade to advance their lot in life.

Speaking of God and the attainment of individual salvation, the churches are preaching social justice instead of the Protestant work ethic. These manmade institutions want to make sure you know that your poverty is not a result of the choices you made, but are the result of the white man, the color of your skin, your accent, your degenerate father, or your helpless mother. Your unfortunate station in life is the result of everyone else deserting and oppressing you. You share none of the responsibility for your station in life, should not seek to change your position and are completely absolved of being in your position. Amen!

The good Progressive liberal teaches that you, black or white, have played no role in becoming poor and therefore you are not the least bit responsible for your status. You are the real victim of oppression. Believe it because the church and your government say it is so and they are now reinforcing each other's position.

The police and their union slave masters also profit from high salaries and fantastic compensation packages just like the teachers. I would say that teachers are different, but in inner city schools they too have to worry about being killed at school on a daily basis just like the police.

The police stay busy protecting the inner city businesses and other law abiding citizens from drugs, theft, robbery and other crimes committed by a second generation of bored, uneducated and poor inner city plantation thugs. These officers are the people we have hired to protect all of us, including the poor from crime.

They are not perceived as fine upstanding public servants in the eyes of the poor or black Americans. They are "da Man." The few police officers that abuse the power and trust of the American people are held up as the norm in the inner city. Even though these rogue officers, protected by the unions, are the exception and not the rule, the poor and more specifically the blacks, believe they are the rule.

I wonder how many rogues officers were socially promoted or protected from dismissal by union contracts. We need to see a study on this possible travesty. It is unfortunate that these rogue officers pay union dues and are contractually protected from legal prosecution. If there is a problem, they will be judged by internal affairs; other police officers. They are judged by a jury of their peers but not in a court of law.

It is a belief in the poor neighborhoods that police are there to racially and socially profile them and make sure they stay in their place. This is what the poor and blacks have been subject to throughout American history. It is what they are taught at home and in school and that is why there is a major lack of respect for law enforcement in the inner city.

The majority of American police officers are upstanding men and women. They should be respected and their service rewarded with adequate compensation. My complaints are not against these officers.

My complaint is against the abuse and ineptitude of unions and government when negotiating with the public purse. My complaint is when unions are allowed any access to the government (taxpayers) employees. Union employment contracting and negotiations should be outlawed for public employees. Unions protect those who need to be removed from service and lower the standards of those who remain to serve.

The inner city culture also appears to attract and protect the degenerates of its society. The police are looked at as the enemy instead of the ones preventing crimes. You are cool if you drop out. It is accepted as normal if you become a pregnant teen. It is even more normal to become pregnant out of wedlock.

The inner city subculture seems to wrap itself around the perversion of gangs and gang violence. Rap music regularly elicits the most disgusting aspects of inner city life. Illicit sex, violence against women, bigotry, race baiting, illegal solicitations of all kinds and random acts of murder are common themes portrayed as art. It is a society of intentional and well designed misfits.

If I were Freud I would think this might be a reflection of being raised by a single parent household, namely the mother. It may be the result of being raised by a secular government, namely a liberal Progressive. We will have to save that for another discussion.

So everyone benefits off the inner city plantation except the resident. She is probably single, had an abortion, has a child, and hasn't completed high school. He may be a gangbanger, probably has at least one child out of wedlock, doesn't pay child support, is unemployed, and hasn't graduated high school. If he has the ambition against all the odds to get out of the plantation, he is only offered a hand out to stay not a hand up to leave.

Yes, all of us in America should be proud to say that we are Americans and my poor, ignorant brother and sister are being paid for through government programs such as Welfare, Medicaid, Food Stamp, and Socialized Medicine. It is the perfect design of the Liberal Progressive Secularist Government and an even more perfect FAILURE! It is by design and implementation the product of the Democrat party plan.

Even though they have constitutional rights afforded every American citizen to succeed, the children in these projects have been brain washed by government schools to believe that government is the best provider. Your parents aren't the best providers and in most inner city cases, that would be your own mother.

You are taught in public school by teachers and community organizers (aftercare programs) that you don't have to do anything and that you are entitled to everything you receive from the government. This is the mantra instilled into all American children in our public schools. Not that you can and should achieve through your efforts, but that you are entitled to any thing you perceive as a need or right simply by being here.

The government schools have purposely lowered the educational standards for the average child. Instead of raising the average child to his or her potential, we have lowered curriculum standards to the mean and further, we have lowered expectations for the exceptional students. Curriculums which historically centered on math, science, and civics are being shelved for classes in diversity training, social justice and environmental studies.

The public schools responsible for our children's education frown on individual achievement and success; no winners and no losers allowed. A socialist norm teaches that everyone is the same and everyone is equal. This is a fallacy and utter nonsense.

Politicians pour money and resources into union offices, school administrative personnel (not teachers)salaries, breakfast, lunch and dinner welfare food programs, as well as feel good programs such as "Participation Day Awards", "Black History Month" or the ever inclusive and diverse, "Bring Your Two Dad's-to-School Day" for show and tell.

As I have stated before and I will continue to hammer this point home; the government is the worst of all parents and the worst of all educators. This is especially true in the inner city schools where poor and often single parents are more dependent on the government for most sustenance. In fact, once the woman has been bred, the man can move on to the next woman and the government will fill the vacuum of father, breadwinner and teacher.

The pregnant young girl, teenager or woman will get additional stipends for every child she delivers. I don't know about you, but if I had to chose between having a "government father" and being a bastard without a father. The bastard would be the better bet!

I believe abortion approved, encouraged and paid for by the government directly or indirectly is a big problem in America; especially in the black community. The very least it is discriminatory gendered based approved murder.

I think poor single parent families, mostly unwed mothers and deadbeat dads, are trained, enabled and forced to be totally dependent on the government through government entitlement programs such as welfare, day care, SNAP (food stamps), family outreach and abortion clinics. The government is now playing the role of the man, husband, doctor, breadwinner and murder co-conspirator.

Poor women are surrogate parents. They are being used as brood mares, indentured into raising someone else's child. They are raising the government's child. How can this type of servitude be any better than the slavery of the past? Where are the Civil Rights leaders on this issue? Why hasn't the DOJ filed legal proceedings against the federal government on these civil rights issues?

It is a major problem when males are being raised by their mothers and don't receive appropriate discipline, guidance and direction from an actual male father figure. The loss of a father's discipline and guidance is one of the root causes for the increase in the inner city crime rate. This lack of parenting is a result of the dissolution of the extended and nuclear family units. Infections always start at the bottom and work their way to the surface.

The lack of an authoritative or disciplinary role model in child rearing allows a void to fester which encourages disrespect for authority. A role model is needed to foster a positive environment where a child's self-esteem can develop. An authoritarian is also beneficial in teaching children, especially adolescents, self-control, respect for others, and providing limits and consequences for one's actions.

The current Great Depression that we are muddling through and the local, state and federal government's interference in the market place have exasperated an already high rate of black male and black youth unemployment. This economic depression has been caused by many factors.

We have a massive deficit spending. We have a Democrat majority running the Senate that hasn't produced or approved a federal budget for years. We have a tyrannical socialist king in the White House, a complacent dysfunctional House and an activist judiciary destroying America from the top down.

A prime example this irresponsible spending is the open flood gates at the US Treasury funding excessive entitlement programs. This excessive spending is being done by the President, those in his Democrat Party and the Democrat controlled Senate specifically. The excessive dropout rate from our nanny state run daycare-dining hall- inner city education system plagues the black and poor communities. Numerous other entitlement programs bankrupt the government coffers and drag the poor even further into the cultural and economic abyss.

The elected representatives of the federal government have created a new nanny state in America. The government is a tyrannical behemoth that infringes on all of our individual rights and freedoms. It is a mismanaged anchor on the ass of every American which has caused the demise of our world renowned education, health, and retirement systems through its incessant interference and coffer pilfering.

The secular progressives have attacked and trivialized our religious institutions, charities and moral beliefs. Private institutions through time which have provided more assistance to the poor in our society than any government imposed program ever crammed down our throats in America.

This socialist mentality demands the subjugation of the American people by forcing the development of an entitlement society. The individual has no choice once they relinquish their freedoms and liberties to the government.

Freedom allows Individualism, Innovation, Self-Reliance and Self- Determination. These are the precious gifts afforded a truly free people. All governments fear such freedom for Individualism robs the government of their ultimate power; the power of control over the masses.

It is hard to believe our great nation has succumbed to such deviousness and treachery. What was once handled by the independent local communities, churches and charity have been taken over and regulated by the local, state and federal governments. None of which is directly provided for in the US Constitution. All of which has been used to finance a cesspool of theft, waste, corruption and utter dependence.

The federal, state and local government's confiscate taxes from the working private sector and then provides all the public services (housing, health, welfare, education) which would be necessary to <u>control all people</u> not just the poor. The poor are just the experimental lab rats for the liberal progressives. The poor are left in a position of total dependence where they cannot fend for themselves. They are the subjects on whom liberals prey and test their theories and programs.

This is my opinion of all government, "There isn't a single service that the Public Sector (government) can provide as cost effectively, efficiently or with better results than the Private Sector (business) can provide. The "inner city projects" prove my point and are perfect examples of the "Man" keeping everyone down.

Now repeat after me, the "Man" is a member of the liberal, progressive, Democrat Party. The SS, Brown shirts, financiers and thugs for the Democrat Party are the unions, DHS, IRS and the DOJ. These are just a few agencies and groups. There are many others housed within the DC beltway.

Let's discuss unions that organize public employees through the benefits of the taxpayer purse. Public institutions paid for with tax dollars should outlaw union participation. If they are not outlawed at the very least, they should be stripped of all collective bargaining. Being a member of a union is not a labor right, only doled out political privileges. Unions should not be able to negotiate pay contracts or benefits in public institutions with taxpayer dollars. Collective bargaining in public institutions should be abolished.

Unions were originally created to protect the working conditions and worker safety; not negotiate wages. While we are abolishing collective bargaining we should abolish the National Labor Relations Board too! This is a socialist solidarity group of politically appointed cronies if there ever were one. Government should literally and completely stay out of the private sector's business.

The largest benefactor of the car company bailouts and the stimulus packages by the Bush and Obama administrations have been the unions. That's why no jobs were created. Our tax money was used to prop up excessive union retirement accounts that were unreasonable, expensive and underfunded. The car companies were failing because of outrageously generous underfunded Cadillac pension plans and lucrative employee wage/benefits contracts. They should have allowed the companies deemed "to big to fail" to declare bankruptcy and reorganize. The pensions should have been renegotiated, mediated, restructured or preferably eliminated like any other company would have to do.

Our tax money was used to pay huge bonuses to the officers of failed financial institutions such as Fannie Mae. Again, there is no allowance for these bailouts in the Constitution of the United States. It was an abuse of power, both executive and legislative. The taxpayer's money printed out of thin air, then stolen from the treasury to pick and choose who should succeed and who should fail.

One should wonder how many tax dollars went to these organizations and were then used as political donations to fund the Democrat Party? That is for another book at another time. Let's return to one of the liberal progressive's successful welfare programs- the inner city projects.

The federal government has been very successful in building these special inner city projects. They've erected these plantations all over the country; mile after mile and block after block of "Public" housing. The Negroes in America went from southern servitude to federal servitude in less than 100 years.

A new problem was created during this transition to federal servitude. While most poor blacks and poor white people were being forced into federal servitude camps, so were all the other American citizens who's wealth acquired through hard work was being confiscated for taxes and redistributed to pay for the enslaved.

The enslaved class is growing in America under the Democrat plan. Currently, 90 million Americans are unemployed. Instead of a minimal government of and for the people, we have become a people of and for the government and that's down right pathetic and anti-American.

In essence, the blacks are enslaved again, and they are not alone. They are being led by their noses by their bought and paid for false prophets and modern day overseers in the government. We are all unwillingly being forced down this regressive path; a path of intentional design.

The blacks are still not subjugated in the historical sense. There is a new American slavery being provided by the very saviors of the black culture in America-the Democrat Party. This party is firmly entrenched in the demise of America with a perverted vision far removed from the eyes of our founding fathers.

Don't hang your hat on the Democrats plan for salvation. The ants will never work for the grasshopper. The ants will ultimately eat the grasshopper. The inner-city plantations need to be torn down. Section 8 housing and all state and federal government funding for inner city construction and maintenance should be stopped. Close the plantations so that people can rise with a hand up instead of a hand out.

Inner City projects are failed socialist inspired programs of dependency and entitlement that kills any initiatives for progress and success. These socialist and communist programs failed in Eastern Europe and the USSR. They are currently failing in Western Europe. The entire socialist political theory is Anti-American and as destructive to our future as the present day inner city plantations and the southern plantations of the past!

It is time for us to close the inner- city plantations and assimilate all races and cultures into the greater society of America. If there is no assimilation than this and all discussion on these race issues are futile and useless.

You can't really believe that America owes reparations for what occurred 100 years ago. The great thing about America is that the black community can't be forced to assimilate, and they are protected by the very documents that give them and all of us our freedoms. However, in return for those protections and freedoms they have responsibilities for themselves and their fellow Americans.

Black Americans cannot expect all the other Americans to keep looking for ways to eradicate their situation, when they have opportunities afforded to choose a different path. In other countries you would be stripped of your citizenship, subjugated, forced to comply or worse-be killed! American blacks owe it to themselves and to America to jump in the melting pot. They are an intricate and important part of America. It is time to participate in America's resurrection and redemption.

Abolish Quotas, Affirmative Action, Discrimination and Reverse Discrimination

It is my humble opinion that the U.S. Federal Government, the all loving, all knowing and all powerful, champion of social equality and social justice, is actually the biggest racist organization ever created in the history of the world.

They have conceived, designed and instituted divisive programs from their hallowed offices and chambers. The Congress caucuses by party, gender and race. It doesn't discriminate against one race. It divides and discriminates against all races much like our President who intentionally divides Americans along racial, gender and political lines on a daily basis; especially when he swaggers down the runway pandering to his adoring press corp(s).

The federal, state and local governments create and encourage programs of diversity and equality through the imposition of quotas and affirmative action programs. Government and government agencies, such as the US Department of Justice, turn a blind eye toward cases of reverse discrimination or black racism, but has an entire office dedicated to the investigation and prosecution of discrimination against black men or black women. The division of Civil Rights at the DOJ is anything but a blind lady of justice. This lady only sees color all too vividly, and that color is black. But this is what have we come to expect from a race baiting incompetent yellow coward like the current attorney general.

This is not just a black problem. This has snowballed into a race, gender, and transgender problem. These programs didn't start out that way. It was an idea started by liberal elites in academia and government during the Civil Rights era. These programs were put to use during the women's liberation movement of the 1960's too.

Affirmative action was a move to help blacks and women rise to an equal status with whites, especially white men in American society. Promoted by John F. Kennedy and more accurately Bobby Kennedy, both liberal Democrats, affirmative action was introduced in 1965 to promote equal opportunity first for blacks. Later the programs ballooned to include women and then anyone perceived as down trodden and oppressed, like Islamic terrorists today.

Just like his predecessor FDR, Kennedy secured the black and female vote through these types of social engineering programs. If only we could have burned these policies while burning the bras we'd be better off now.

Affirmative action was perceived as necessary for women to "transcend" their traditional roles of wife, mother and matriarch. These programs would allow women to leave their traditional roles and join the work force traditionally held by men. These programs encouraged young ladies in all social classes to pursue their goals through access and acceptance into colleges and universities.

It was a system established to bring equality of pay scales based on job performance instead of discrimination based on sex or color. It allowed women to break through the "glass ceiling." Basically, it promoted and fostered women taking on the roles traditionally held by men, making it acceptable to choose other career paths there by relinquishing many of their traditional roles in American society.

Affirmative action and quotas were also used to make sure that blacks were not denied advancement due to race. These are all good motives and well intentioned. However, the playing fields were not leveled by government. They were tilted in the opposite direction. In fact, the result has been reverse discrimination and the lowering of work standards.

The negative results of these programs far outweigh any benefits for American society overall. Like all good intentions, these government assistance programs were soon corrupted by excessive and regressive practices.

The legal system crammed the courts with frivolous lawsuits. Reverse discrimination became rationalized and accepted as justification for any form of inequality. This was brainwashed into our youth by our public and college education systems. Government control and oppression was imposed on the white male just like slavery. It is still being practiced to this day.

These programs did not promote equality. They promoted the lowering of American standards of excellence to accommodate gender pacification and a race of people deprived for decades of a quality public education. Admission requirements were changed and lowered. Quotas were instituted to insure and secure access to these educational institutions even if the students admitted were subpar.

I want to say one thing about this perverse period of enlightenment known to the baby boomers as the 1960's. This should go down in American history as the worst decade in American history. It was the extinction of the extended family unit. It was the beginning of the end for the nuclear family.

During this period America introduced us to gender confusion under the banner of live and let live. It was the rebirth of socialism and communism disguised under the cloak of the Progressive Liberal movement which had spilled out of the halls of academia and raised its ugly head as a festering sore in the polluted bowels of the Democrat party.

It was the degenerate decade of the 1960's that set the stage for the current political battles between leftists and conservatives today. The losers from that decade ended up becoming today's professors, academic elites, filling the professorships at our most prestigious universities and advancing their Secular/Socialist curricula through higher education. It was a dark and turbulent period which accelerated to warp speed the moral decline in America on a number of fronts. That will have to be a discussion for another time. Suffice it to say, the destructive cancer infecting America now was created during this period in history.

The reasons for implementing Affirmative Action Programs appear to have been honorable and noble. They were an attempt by government and other public institutions to level the playing field between blacks and whites and men and women. As with all good intentions placed in the hands of the politicians in public institutions such as government or schools, they fail. This is the same in all countries and by all forms of governments.

Why? Because when it comes to politics or public education, only certain things matter. For politicians, they have to secure votes. Votes are the path to financial wealth and a confirmation by their constituency giving them power over the people. In order to be a successful politician, they have to appeal to the masses and not to the individual. It is quantity over quality which is exactly what you can say about the politicians we have in office now.

First the politicians had to throw money at the problem and the beneficiaries of those funds were originally black Americans and women. The base has expanded considerably now to include Hispanics, Asians, Transgenders, homosexuals, ex-cons, children and of course, the physical or mentally handicapped.

I don't really know why the ex-cons have joined the club because they can't vote unless they are Democrats and live in Al Franken's state, Missouri or in the city of Chicago. I throw children in just because you know how much politicians love the children and their parents are a voting bloc too! But rest assured, some politician is benefiting off the Affirmative Action dole somewhere.

Who else gains from affirmative action programs? Local, State and Federal employees have to be somewhat qualified in spite of union intervention. Yes, this includes all the public servants whose salaries and compensations are paid for by the taxpayer. You know, teachers, police, and the lady behind the desk at the driver's license bureau. Once they have jumped a few pre-qualification hurdles they are on the dole and in for life with guaranteed promotions and Cadillac retirement plans.

It is almost impossible to fire them. Even if you are a pedophile in a New York City classroom, they can't or won't fire you. They keep paying you and then send you to a special building in downtown Manhattan with all the other government certified teaching pedophiles.

The opposite of affirmative action is reverse or what I call regular discrimination. Here we have another one of those pesky issues. You can't be discriminated against if you are any color, sex, unisex, transex, homosex, ex-con, child, handicapped or a war hero; EXCEPT IF YOU ARE A WHITE MALE! Then it's not discrimination or racism. The new definition of a racist is primarily that you be a white male. It is totally acceptable to everyone if you are willing to accept it. I am not.

This is why our government can't institute affirmative action programs, quotas etc. It is completely incompetent and ill equipped to be fair and just. It never achieves its intended goals because of this simple fact. We are not all equal and the government can't make a square peg go through a round hole. However, if the real intent is to divide us, then affirmative action programs and quotas have proven extremely successful.

Think about it and be honest. Have we lowered the standard requirements of the Presidency in order to elect the first black president? Is race more important than upholding the principles of our founding fathers that have been so beautifully preserved for us in the US Constitution and Bill of Rights?

Why wasn't the President vetted by the media? Why weren't his grades and transcripts released to the public? Has he been a recipient of benefits from affirmative action or race based quota programs? Was Barack Obama ever socially promoted in school due to race? Am I going to be labeled a racist for asking these questions? Remember the old saying, "Ye who protest too much!" The closer one gets to the truth, the stronger will grow the resistance.

Would the media give Al Sharpton or Jesse Jackson Sr. a bully pulpit to self- promote if their messages didn't promote faux oppression and victimhood? So what if they marched with Rev. King. Let's face it, they are not Rev. King.

They are just as responsible if not more so for the racial divide in this country then those they condemn and mock. They detest racial profiling but they encourage programs of affirmative action and reverse discrimination. These too are forms of racial profiling. These men are classic hypocrites.

It is unfortunate that they ride on the coat tail of an iconic minister of peace and then feel entitled through incidental personal association to spew diatribes of racism, racial profiling, and the promotion of limited free speech by calling any speech they don't agree with hate speech. What exactly is the definition of prostitution? Is it gender specific or can it be performed from the podium and pulpit?

These racist activists continue to inflict divisive rhetoric on the black communities seeking never ending reparations for a time long past. Their actions are as much a growing cancer on the face of America as slavery is a scar.

These political pundits, labor union bosses and community organizers, use race baiting and class baiting to accomplish their missions day in and day out. They endorse affirmative action programs and implement them for the benefit of their union members. They use these programs to gain the votes of blacks and women. If the unions and politicians didn't do this, they wouldn't be relevant to their political base. They couldn't get elected without this dog and pony show, because they have a fatally flawed platform requiring government dependency. They promote complete chaos amongst the American electorate; a slight of hand.

President Obama has openly proposed to dismantle the entire American structure through the socialist ideology of "wealth redistribution". Like all forms of discrimination or the practice of picking winners and losers, the redistribution program is a union and Democrat Party tool. It is blatant financial, racial and gender discrimination.

Working Americans are not just going to freely give everything they worked for away to a tyrannical president and statist form of government to be squandered on the moochers. Those who promote wealth redistribution should lead by example. Honestly, those who promote wealth distribution should not be considered fit for office, more or less be allowed to lead anything or anyone in America.

Affirmative action and quotas are funded through this redistribution ideal. This concept requires the confiscation of wealth from one to be redistributed to another chosen by the government. The confiscated taxes are used to fund and subsidize these programs. Those who are subsidized return their gratitude with their vote. Their votes are bought with tax dollars and a vicious circle begins.

This is why the original US Constitution required that a person owned property before they could vote. This would stop the politicians and the moochers from stealing from the US Treasury. Those who pay taxes and practice their right to vote are less likely to vote for people who use those confiscated taxes for Affirmative action, quotas and other welfare programs. The idea of owning property would assure that the US Treasury would remain solvent and the power of the taxpayer's purse would be protected from theft by the producers filling it.

Why would one rob from oneself? The founding fathers knew exactly what they were doing. By constitutionally requiring that a white male had to own property before they were eligible to vote, the voter had to have a real vested interest in our nation. Now you can plainly see how the "evolution" of the Constitution by the liberal progressive has been truly regressive to the health of our nation.

This clause in the constitution was legislated out of existence overtime by state and federal voting laws. Laws were passed giving all Americans of legal age the right to vote regardless of religion, race, and sex. These amendments and laws led to the repeal of the property ownership requirements. Government legislated and created numerous laws that chiseled away any protections from theft of the US Treasury by the political class and their moocher base. It was not voted on by the people. It was legislated out of the constitution and into history.

The elimination of the personal property requirement opened the Treasury purse to pandering politicians and special interests groups. The result is that taxes collected since have been misappropriated to buy votes and fund entitlement programs. Like manure, the tax dollars were redistributed in return for a moochers vote. This is the system in which we operate today.

The proponents of all redistribution programs should be the first to be stripped of all their assets. Their accumulated wealth, annual incomes and all savings should be confiscated and placed on deposit with the US Treasury. The money on deposit will be used to reimburse all the monies stolen from Social Security and Medicare, which have been misappropriated and redirected from the Treasury to fund other government welfare programs. The remainder of any leftover funds taken from the political proponents of redistribution would then be held on deposit as a penalty for the mismanagement and abuse of their fiduciary responsibilities to the American people.

For the liberal regressives who are the champions of wealth confiscation and redistribution, their penalty funds will be used to pay down our massive debt incurred due to their failed socialist plans. Finally, both the broke democrats and the broke far-left socialist liberals should be forcibly moved into the inner city and be made to live off what they have created. In one generation the democrat party, degenerate politicians and socialist libertards would peacefully die off into oblivion.

Redistribution is necessary to fund welfare programs which in turn guarantees people will stay in poverty while securing the Democrat vote. It is the financial reward skimmed off the top used to fill the pockets of Democrats. It is rhetoric espoused by politicians and pulpit pushers to promote discriminatory practices such as affirmative action, quotas and welfare. But more importantly and sadly, it is a major financial and personal burden put on the backs of what is left of the hard working American middle class.

It seems the liberal far left in the Democrat party use the same playbook whenever they want to pull one over on the American people. They accomplish their goals through division, diversion and deception. They lower all the standards through their regressive social programs and education curriculums. Once this is accomplished, they pander to the ignorant and lowest members of the American populace which they have intentionally shackled in poverty.

Democrats/Socialists, especially the Obama administration, use class, gender and race warfare, aided and abetted by a cheerleading mass and multi-media ready and willing to spread its propaganda. If they aren't aggressively promoting the socialist agenda like MSNBC, they are at the very least complacent in their reporting.

In order for the far-left liberal to succeed, government has to seize the <u>earned</u> wealth of the producers through fees and taxation, and then give it to the non- producing moochers in our society. If the US Treasury could not be raided to pay for these social justice programs, the Democrat party would cease to exist. No honest, intelligent and hard working American would ever vote for them. No honest, intelligent and hard working American taxpayer would allow the corruption and abuse of the system to continue.

Lowering the standards and qualifications of employees while negotiating and over paying them through excessive compensation is how affirmative action is procured by our socialist brothers in the unions. Unions were created to provide a safe work environment. The dues generated were to be used for displaced workers or workers who couldn't work because of a work related injuries. The dues were never intended to be used as vote payments or political bribes. What is the saying about money corrupting completely?

But since the union bosses found that they could use union dues to pay politicians instead of fund membership benefits, they too have become corrupted and shamelessly participate in the corrupt politics of the Democrat Party to securing ill gotten benefits for their members. They have evolved into despicable socialists party thugs who are taking their place in line at the trough of the tax payers, like the President they serve.

These unions are SEIU, the AFL-CIO and many other federal, state and local government unions representing employees; postal workers, teachers, police and firefighters. It is not the professional members that are reprehensible. In many cases they are required to be union members in order to work in their field. It is the paid union leadership and full time employees of union's management who grease the pockets of the politicians. They are the ones who are to be singled out and investigated for corruption, tax evasion, voter fraud and vote tampering.

Working with the progressive far-left politicians, they redistribute confiscated wealth from the taxpayer through collective bargaining for their public employees. The redistribution of wealth in this fashion is its own form of financial affirmative action.

Union leaders negotiate with elected officials executing lucrative employment contracts and Cadillac pension plans on the backs of the taxpayers. Since affirmative action lowers standards to the least common denominator in any profession, you can say that unions are required to incorporate these socialist programs into their employment guidelines thereby lowering quality and standards.

Unions hire these employees with your tax dollars thereby forcing substandard employees and services on the tax payer. In return, the best employee for the job is passed over because the best applicant exceeds the necessary requirements to get the job. The lowering of overall standards is a negative net result of income redistribution at the over burdened expense of the taxpayer.

As previously stated, this is not an attack on the professional teachers, firefighters etc. It is the union bosses and the political hacks that are to blame. A person would be a fool not to jump on these publically funded gravy trains. Unfortunately and regrettably, the excessive taxes required to fund these unions are bankrupting the country.

In return for their political favors and patronage, unions actively work for this administration and the Democrat party. The ground support provided by these political subversive operatives are openly endorsed and encouraged by the Obama administration and are major sources of campaign funds for the DNC. The Democrat campaign chests are full of union dues in the form of political contributions. Why else would the president entertain union bosses like Stern and Trumpka at the White House so many times?

What group's pension plans were fully funded with tax payer dollars when Obama bailed out GM? The unions benefited and sent their tax payer bailout funds right back to the Democrat campaign coffers. Was General Motors too big to fail or would the loss of campaign dollars adversely affect the election and the President's chances of re-election. Follow the money, Right?

I believe the tax money used for the bailout directly or indirectly flowed to the unions and back to the president's re-election campaign. The tally of our losses on that debacle are still not complete, because the US Treasury still owns stock in General Motors as of the publishing of this book.

The President didn't even have to stop golfing due to the union protests, mayhem and riots which took place in Oakland, Wisconsin, Wall Street or Washington during his first term. He wasn't concerned because the union members present were there for him and they represented socialist ideals and communist solidarity which the President supports. Of course, most of the degenerates urinating and raping during these protests were also Democrat supporters.

The union arm of the Democrat Party is representative of flagrant political cronyism and corruption prevalent in all politics today. It is one more example of the great successes we have achieved through the use of affirmative action programs. The unions promote lower standards of achievement, protect the worst in their ranks and we elect panderers instead of leaders.

The current mayor of Chicago, Rahm Emanuel, stated when he was chief of staff for President Obama, not to waste the political opportunities that arise during a crisis. These leaders sensationalize and exaggerate stories of police discrimination and the use of racial profiling when the real problem is that hundreds of inner city murders and crimes are taking place in their streets because they can't profile criminals. If it looks like a pig and smells like a pig, it's a pig!

The Civil Rights Movement was a movement to assimilate blacks into the American culture and move forward. It was a movement to bring Americans together. It was not meant to be a white apology tour.

Police officers are hired to protect and serve. They are discriminated against in the black community by those blacks they have been hired to protect and serve. But this is not a bias of color. It is a bias by color. Many black people do not trust or respect law enforcement plain and simple.

It is a lesson taught in black culture, passed down by black people to black people. Place the blame squarely on this culture that encourages the distrust and disregard for law enforcement. No, that would require a mirror, and it makes for better TV to riot over the misconduct of a few rogue cops or murder a neighbor who is in a different gang than to look at one's self to see the problem.

There could be another reason for inappropriate police behavior. It may be that the quality of the officer hired in Chicago is sub-par. We already know that diversity programs and other social experiments do not work. See how many rogue officers were hired in order to fulfill the requirements of affirmative action, quotas, gender, or kept on the force because of union employment contracts that make it legally impossible or cost prohibitive to get these sub-standard officers off the force.

The socialist liberal Democrat biggest fear is for the public to unite and rise against them like our founding fathers did against the tyranny of England. If they keep us fighting amongst ourselves, then they can make progress with their destructive agenda. The final outcome is to morph us into some quasi-socialist western European/communist state. The plan is to divide and conquer, old school but highly effective as you can see today's political environment. If We the People become too unruly, the president will just call out his national police force; the Department of Homeland Security.

One common objective of socialism /communism and there social programs is to make everyone equal. That is why we have spent fortunes formulating and adjudicating affirmative action plans. At the very least, they try to make it appear that we are all equal.

Politicians, especially liberally regressives, attempt to reach this goal through the manipulation of the electorate. They keep the classes divided by rewarding the below average and average while punishing the exceptional. Their final goal is to make sure that no one is exceptional but equal. Of course, the socialist leaders are exempt from this socially imposed equality. They will be exceptional, wealthy and have absolute power over you.

People need to understand and realize there will never be equality. There will always be greater and lesser persons than yourself; familiarize yourself with Desiderata. If nothing else, take the time to familiarize yourself with the laws of nature; you know "survival of the fittest" and anatomically different.

We may achieve <u>sameness</u>, but we will never achieve equality. There have been many attempts to enforce and force equality. All of these socially engineered plans have failed and the dysfunctional remnants or unintended consequences are dragging our country down daily.

Affirmative action, quotas and reverse discrimination are "feel good" placebos sold to a publicly educated and thereby their ignorant populace. These programs have taken on a life of their own. They have run amok and need to be abolished.

They were created to show white empathy for past racial, gender and other socially perceived injustices. It is difficult to empathize with someone who wasn't a victim of some past injustice; only an inheritor of the injustice. It is totally queer. Federal, state and local government programs imposed on the basis of equality and leveling the playing field will always fail. Those governed the least are governed best.

In our world, the United States Federal Government is the newest and biggest type of slave owner on the planet. These diversity programs are tools to promote confusion and achieve individual submission. The government is trying to control every aspect of our lives. What makes this government any different than the plantation owner of the South prior to the Civil War? Absolutely nothing is different and this slavery is just as abhorrent.

In a previously televised speech, President Obama stated the American public was unqualified (stupid) and that "*he*" and other professional politicians are smarter, better qualified and in a better position to run the government on our behalf. He was absolutely and completely condescending. He does come across sometimes to be a nice guy, but he doesn't seem to be as brilliant as some profess and often time comes off as very narcissistic.

But what do you expect when you have a bunch of guilt ridden white liberals in the media and in your party fawning over the first example of a mixed race affirmative action success story. It shouldn't be important that a President be a specific color or gender. It is however imperative that he have the qualities and experience of a good leader. It is important that he represents all Americans not just his party, his donors or his race-white, black or blue. There are other affirmative action success stories to be found I am sure, but not at the level of the Presidency.

Sometimes you are just a lowly female Supreme Court Justice. You're really lucky if you are super qualified enough to hold the office by being both a Latino and a woman. This superior justice would have two affirmative groups to mark on her affirmative action resume. You can enlighten all of us by your unique experiences and perspectives of being Latin and a woman; both obvious classes of victimhood in America.

Unlike old white men, you are uniquely qualified for your position as US Supreme Court Justice by the mere fact that you are a minority, Latin, and a Woman. Those superior race-gender specific qualifications are evidently the more important requirements necessary to land you a lifetime seat on the highest court in the land. You don't even have to be the best lawyer, just an oppressed member of the victimhood class.

The state schools (local elementary, middle, high schools and colleges) receive federal funding if you socially promote students through the use of quotas and other progressive programs. In essence, the schools are graded according to how many students they push through to graduation. These benefits to the schools are not just financial. They include food, water, clothing, condoms and daycare (for the really ignorant students who get pregnant) provided that the schools comply with all required federal mandates.

Although this section may be tinged with sarcasm or politically safe and acceptable use of satire, it exemplifies how the most noble of intentions when mismanaged by the government and mandated through public institutions create the perfect conditions for failure.

The President's rapid accent in academia may have little to do with his supposed brilliance and is most likely the result of some form of liberally designed academic social promotion program. We don't know because his records are sealed. Maybe he was moved ahead in school to fulfill a biracial children quota or single mom quota. Frankly, you don't know a lot about the man in general unless you like golf. One can only assume his educational achievements are valid with the limited information available. It took years to produce a birth certificate. How long will it take before he releases his academic record?

The liberal public and media grovel at his feet and use his rise to the presidency as a vindication for the sins of white America's past. (Alleluia and Praise the Lord! Yes Jesus, not Barry!) None of these scenarios are acceptable reasons to elect him to the highest office in the land or the position of the most powerful man in the world.

His whole career has been achieved by pandering to the inner city residents and working with the overseers in community organizing groups. He is the poster child of a mixed race marriage, survivor of a broken home, raised out of poverty against all odds; the perfect story line for the making of a hallmark channel special. They don't seem to be the best qualifications or requirements necessary to be the commander and chief of the United States.

No conspiracy theories are lurking between the lines of this book. However, the little we know about this man and his past raises one's curiosity a bit. Why wasn't this president completely vetted by the media? Why haven't his appointees been vetted fully by the media? How and for what reasons have his affiliations with home grown terrorists, Muslim sympathizers and communists been minimized and swept under the rug? Everyone knows if you lay down with dogs you get up with fleas.

Any other President would be hammered day and night by the press if he/she associated with these derelicts. Every other president in American history has received more scrutiny than this president. Is everyone turning a blind eye to protect the legacy of the first black President after Bill Clinton? Is it to give these programs some claim of success so the Democrat Party can justify their continued existence? So the politicians can continue to control the ballot box and raid the treasury?

I wouldn't put anything past those who have expressed their desire to "fundamentally transform" my country. I would not trust those who would like to create chaos by dismantling my country upside down, inside out, bottom up and top down. This intentional and internally controlled dismantling by the executive branch, the Senate and the democrat party at large is my definition of high treason. It is not progress.

All actions taken by the political elite to divide and separate people by class, gender or race should be illegal in America. Affirmative action should be illegal and should be outlawed for being discriminatory to one race and one gender. America is better than this!

This was the very core of the Civil Rights movement; to rise up and bring together a divided America. It was an era to seek equal justice for all Americans. At least, that is the bill of goods we were sold at the time.

Affirmative action programs and quotas are tools used by liberals to advance the ideas of social justice; to provide to each according to one's needs under the illusion of equality. They elevate the term, special privileges to being the same as personal or civil "rights" to a delineated class of people who are perceived as victims. Everybody is a victim.

Blacks are victims. Women are victims. Gay people are victims. Frankly, the only people who aren't victims are white American males, unless they are gay or transgendered. *This proves my point that only white males are not allowed to be victims in America.*

Many of the laws and regulations that are being instituted are not to protect the social deviants or deviant classes in our society from the oppression of the majority. They are being created to force their deviant ways of life on the majority and make them morally acceptable to the majority. They want their deviance to be made relevant and acceptable to the majority.

The minority is trying to socially engineer the natural biological laws of nature through legislative and judicial activism. This attempt at social engineering through the legislative process is expected to legally force the majority of Americans to accept deviant behavior even if the majority finds the behavior immoral and offensive.

Abortion, same sex marriage, legalization of drugs, healthcare, illegal alien reforms are all examples of minority positions legislated by government over reach thus circumventing the vote of the majority. It is legislative pandering to a minority base. These laws are always defeated when voted on by the public-at-large. However, when legislated, they are forced on the majority by state/federal legislatures or overturned by judicial activist in court. The majority vote is circumvented or over turned through legislative or judicial actions. At the very least, such actions legislatively or judicial imposed against the majority should be challenged as unconstitutional either by state or federal law.

Again, this is a case where the minority would like to be accommodated by the majority instead of assimilating with the majority. Assimilation is the closest thing we have in America to equality. I imagine this promotion of deviant behavior as normal is the same secular thought and evolution that brought about the debauchery, hedonism and the final demise of Sodom and Gomorrah. Is history repeating itself?

We need to abolish the practices of affirmative action, social promotion, reverse discrimination, discrimination, diversity training and quotas. All are horrible programs if not in concept, definitely in practice.

Affirmative action is the process of lowering standards, whether physical or mental, in order to right a wrong committed sometime in the past; a form of reparations for past inequities. In actuality, these social programs double down on the very inequities they were created to eliminate.

Those on the far left will call it leveling the playing field or giving a hand out or making it more "fair" for some oppressed class. It's accelerated welfare pure and simple. It is the accelerated destruction of the middle class in America. It is the acceleration of ignorance through the lowering of education standards and the lowering of individual expectations at a rapid pace.

There is another way to look at it too. What it actually equates to is the process of lowering the expectations and qualities of life for many for the benefit of a few. Affirmative action is rewarding someone for their lack of ability or drive to perform at an equal or advanced level.

We recently applied these programs when appointing the last two US Supreme Court Justices. This is understandable if you are a uniquely qualified Latino woman living in a white man's world or if you feel the US Constitution is not to be taken literally, but as a guideline to evolving law. It is incomprehensible that you would expect only the best and brightest legal scholars to have a seat on the highest court in the land.

Evolving allows you to achieve your ends by letting right be wrong and wrong be right. Evolving is not black or white, it's gray and through this test you can legally change the meaning and intent of a document or word to fit your purpose. "I did not have sex with that woman!" This however flies in the face of truth which is; *all things are black and white and there will never be equality.*

Affirmative action is an unwarranted reward for inaction or ineptitude. Unions protect this type of behavior all the time. Union members are promoted for their lack of responsibility, lack of ability, lack of self-promotion or lack of superior performance.

In regards to reverse discrimination, the same principles apply. The exceptional are held back or passed over because he worked and excelled beyond his lesser contemporaries so he is punished for his success.

The liberal believes that it is not morally acceptable to pass someone over who is inferior or under qualified. You may hurt their feelings and then you would be subject to anti-bullying laws or be sent off to some diversity training camp until you acknowledge the error of your ways; how Orwellian!

As long as you enable someone and reinforce their mental crutch, you do that person a great disservice. When you promote someone based on their "rights" to unearned entitlements, you are rewarding failure and encouraging socialist ideology. You are promoting failure and killing the ambition to improve and progress. The entire quagmire is against nature.

You are in fact, thwarting all desire to improve one's position which will leave one stagnant or subject to regress. The inner city plantations need to be closed, the welfare faucets turned off permanently and all races and creed in America need to truly meld and assimilate under the philosophies and principles that the founding fathers proposed.

There will always be greater and lesser persons, and although we may be the same, we will never be equal individually. There will always be rich and poor. A certificate of participation is not going to make you equal with someone who excels past you. It is nothing but a patch for a deflated and bruised ego. The real injustice perpetrated against any person is when a person is not required to rise up to one's potential and is expected to accept lower standards of success.

It is not the average American citizen that keeps the black man down. The black man shares a lot of the blame. The black leaders share most of the blame. It has been many years since slavery, yet that dead horse gets trotted out regularly.

There have been billions of tax dollars confiscated and then doled out by Democrats buying the black vote under the guise of leveling the playing field. Black Americans have literally been purchased and hood winked by the party. You have been purchased and contained into a mini-nanny state within the larger American culture. It is by socialist design. It is by Democrat design. It is the equivalent of living in an inner-city plantation. Since the black community refuses to assimilate and move up and out, all attempts and programs to fix their problems have failed over and over again.

It is the Democrat Party that benefits from keeping the black man down. It is the Democrat Party that benefits from keeping the electorate ignorant and poorly educated. It is the Democrat Party who benefits from encouraging murder through abortion. It is the Democrat Party that promotes, practices and benefits from class and race division. It is the Democrat Party that introduced America to affirmative action. It is the Democrat Party that promotes the political platform of socialism. It is a vicious circle and it appears to be the basis for these pesky discussions.

I will tell you one more thing that also appears to be happening. The average American citizen is tired of the division, tired of having their tax dollars squandered and huge debts placed on the backs of their children to pay for failed programs and corrupt and inept leaders.

They are tired of government interference and government's attempts at social engineering. This is what has given birth to the Tea Party movement and the awakening of the moderate and conservative American citizen. This is what is making conservatives standup and demand the return of America back to the individual American citizen.

In America, all of us regardless of race, creed or color has the opportunity to reach his or her potential. There is no other country in the world whose founding documents guarantee her people those rights. We are truly at a crossroad of self reliance or total dependency on the state. What's your choice?

Slavery throughout the World

Slavery is a vile institution that has plagued the world since the beginning of time. There were slaves in Mesopotamia, Egypt, Europe, Asia, all over Africa and the rest of the civilized world. Slaves and indentured servants traveled with Columbus and Cortez on their voyages to the New World. Slavery is still practiced in many countries around the world.

The victors of war enslaved or sold the losers of war into slavery. Africans tribes sold other defeated African tribes into slavery. They were purchased and shipped to the Caribbean and the United States. Slavery still exists in many foreign countries including Africa but it manifests itself differently today. No matter how the progressives try to spin it in America, it is still slavery; even if employed under the guise of wealth redistribution. Just like abortion and euthanasia are masked as justifiable murder, slavery is still being practiced and is just as reprehensible.

People in socialist and communist's countries such as China, North Korea, Greece, and Venezuela are controlled and enslaved by their monarchs, dictators, prime ministers, theocrats and politburos. If the regressive liberal socialists in America succeed, we will soon join their ranks.

The poor classes in those countries do not enjoy the rights, freedoms and liberties afforded us in America. Even the poorest of Americans still have the rights afforded by our creator and professed in the US Constitution. The founding documents, the US Constitution and the Bill of Rights, guarantee all Americans these rights.

There is a growing number of political elitist who are being impeded in their attempts to fundamentally transform our country because of these timeless documents. These documents are the basic solid roadblock to a socialist agenda.

Our poor would represent the wealthiest 1% in many third world countries. Our poor can't even recognize what true poverty is. There are no cars, I Phones, IPods, radios or TV's in third world countries. Food is their most important luxury and it's not at a drive thru and it's no longer secured through a government entitlement program. The political elites have become wealthy and absorb all the resources that the producers produce. This leaves no money in their treasuries in which to fund entitlement programs. Therefore, the poor are truly destitute and our inner city plantations look like posh resorts compared to the slums in third world countries thanks to the Progressives.

Visit Port Au Prince Haiti and see how their government provides food for them. The billions of dollars in aid given by the United States has been stolen and squandered by the political class in that country. Their shanties have no windows, walls and dirt floors. They have no food, medicine or adequate shelter. Socialist, fascist and communist progressives govern these countries and they can only remove their leaders by revolt and bloodshed. We in America have the ballot box and justice wielded through common law.

Think of all the huge inner city plantations and slums that blanket Mexico, Central and South America. In those countries the middle class doesn't exist. Their rich are politically powerful and accumulate considerable financial wealth. The state is inherently dependent on the less fortunate, they propagandize the poor, educate and indoctrinate them into believing that they are totally dependent on the state and the state will provide all they need. They do not fulfill their promises. This is where we are headed in America if we haven't already arrived.

Basically, the people in those foreign countries are totally dependent on government for what little sustenance they receive. The government in return requires their votes and political allegiance. The people don't have a choice. Don't fool yourselves into thinking that there are no classes or social strata in foreign countries- democratic, theocratic, socialistic or communists. There are extremely rich and extremely poor with nothing in between.

This is why so many countries are jealous of America. The middle class in America is her pillar of strength. Both the rich and the poor suck off the labor and accumulated earned wealth of the middle class. The people in foreign countries want our freedoms and form of government, but they have no chance of achieving it because they are already under the tyranny of state control.

Communist and socialist countries are bastions for the social justice movement where the individual is nothing but a small cog in a big wheel. You have no rights individually. All rights are inherently the state's rights. The state passes those rights out as favors to those who will support them. The state is dependent on you individually, but misleads you to believe that you are totally dependent on the state.

Again, you have to understand that the people in these countries are completely provided for by their governments for their sustenance and livelihoods. There is no route to change your station in life. Once you succumb and become a ward of the socialist state, it is impossible to return to a democratic republic and regain your individual rights. You are no longer an individual; you are a dependent ward of the state.

There are simply too many insurmountable barriers to overcome when your dependence on the state is absolute. This is the reason why it is nearly impossible to get out of the inner city plantations through government designed and instituted programs. These programs are tools to obtain the objectives of the progressive socialist state. They are by intentional design a coercive way to maintain and contain people at a certain station in life.

But I have to say emphatically that you have a chance and choice to change your circumstances in America due to your freedoms and liberty. If we ever lose these rights we will not have any chance for individual improvement. Once we give up a right to our government, we never get it back. This is a fact. How many freedoms and rights did we relinquish to our government in the Patriot Act? How many of those rights have been abused by the government and how many of those rights have been returned to the people? Not one.

There are classes of rich and poor in all foreign countries regardless of political ideology. There will always be rich and poor. If there are more poor blacks than whites or Hispanics or Asian, then maybe as Michael Jackson said, "Look at the Man in the Mirror." If you can isolate the problem then you have half the solution.

Don't constantly be looking for others to blame for your station in life and don't expect help from a Democrat. Black Americans gave and continue to give the liberals politicians and race baiters their power by staying in the station into which they have been placed. The black American has to remain oppressed and a victim of their society in order for the Democrats to continue to have control over them, a victim whom to pander and a divisive vehicle to create chaos.

I think the liberals and far left in our government create the majority of our problems. They want to keep the American people divided by race. They want to pit white man against black man. This pandemonium keeps our eyes off of the devious politicians who are dismantling our nation. It keeps our eyes off the myriad of scandals plaguing our nation.

No offense to all the people of color, but we whites have enough problems of our own. We don't need to be the scapegoat for inept political pulpit pushers and made to atone for your problems. Pull yourself up by your own boot straps. The white population in America isn't responsible for everyone else's problems, unless you are of the mind set of some maternal social justice advocate.

The federal government is the only group of institutions in America practicing slavery today. The abuse of political power, the political greed and the exploitation of the working middle class by government guarantees the failure of any nation. No society has ever fallen from an economy based on capitalism; they have however fallen by government mismanagement and corruption.

The only way our country can fail is from the same things that have been the demise of all past societies-the abuse of political power by government, political greed, theft of the treasury by those in government, and exploitation of the working class by government. Does any of this seem familiar to you? History does repeat itself.

The academic elites and liberal progressives continue to base their curriculums on socialist theories and programs that have been tried and tested throughout time; miserably failing in every instance. The same experiments getting the same results at the expense of the American people I am sad to say.

We need to let our European neighbors continue to experiment and practice socialist theory. We do not need to implement this political disaster on the American people. We need to free the brain trusts in America to invent and produce new and exciting products for our market. What we really need to do is reinstitute conservative economic policies and principles into government.

We need to dramatically reduce the size and scope of the American federal, state and local governments and allow the private sector to fix all of the government's mistakes. That is a really tall order, but it can be accomplished but only in America while she is still able to recover. We need to free the people from progressive democrat's slavery in order to achieve these goals.

America's scars are literally written into her Constitution and so are her corrections. You can't say that about any other country in the world. Slavery was protected in the Constitution and it was abolished in the Constitution.

Rightly or wrongly, every American citizen has been given the right to vote in federal elections. We can't control what is happening in the rest of the world, but we can control what happens here in America. It is our responsibility to clean the blemish of inner city life off the face of America. This needs to be accomplished through local efforts and not through federal government use of draconian entitlement programs.

Now is the time. America has righted her wrongs for slavery at a huge costs of life, liberty and treasure. She has survived the fighting of a bloody Civil War, a turbulent reconstruction period, an even more contemptuous Civil Rights era; it is time to move forward.

Slavery in America was abolished so let's get over it and move on. Break the bonds of government slavery today in America. Return her to her rightful place protecting the rights and pursuits of happiness guaranteed every individual American by the US Constitution and the Bill of Rights. We have more pressing problems to contend with which threaten the very existence of our great nation. They lay at the feet of the Socialist Progressive deep in the recesses of the Democrat Party.

I am not trying to minimize or trivialize the black and white problem in America, but there are more important and pressing issues that need to be addressed in America. One of those issues is religion.

America is at her core a Christian nation. Even though other cultures and religions enjoy the freedoms afforded every American by the US Constitution and the Bill of Rights, we are predominately a Christian nation. The doctrines of Christianity are weaved into the American fabric all the way to our very foundation.

If you read the Constitution it states that the government will not create a religion nor prohibit the practice of any religion under the 1st Amendment. The separation clause, as it is commonly called, has been politically misinterpreted. The use of misinterpretation is another progressive way to say "evolve" or make black and white "equal" or grey.

Just because sleazy lawmakers, a secular media or some "brilliant" college professors have intentionally misinterpreted or allowed the meaning of the Constitution and Bill of Rights to "evolve" in order to further their causes, does not mean they are correct or that you have to believe or abide by their deceit. You have the perfect right to practice your religion anytime and anywhere you wish and you do not need to obey any laws which would abridge this freedom. You can do it constitutionally and legally, unlike our President and the DOJ who do so illegally and unconstitutionally.

Those serving in the federal government have been acting outside the authority afforded them in the US Constitution for quite some time. This is a very dangerous position for the American people. If the balance of power in government is not kept in check, uncontrollable corruption and abuse will fill the vacuum; the American populace will be the final victims. This is what the American people are witnessing now.

The murders and cover-up in Benghazi, the oppressive illegal tactics of the IRS and the NSA illegally spying on individual Americans with blanket warrants from secret FISA courts should make every blue blooded American stand up and take notice.

The Executive, Legislative and even the judicial branch of the federal government, have been changing the intent and interpretations of the Constitution to fit their agendas. The Constitution interferes and hinders their ability to socially engineer the changes they want in America. Therefore, they must change it, misinterpret it to their benefit or disregard it completely waiting for justice from an incompetent judiciary to catch up. There is no shortage of activist's judges ready and willing to make these interpretations on behest of the progressives. Presently, there are many in the Democrat Party who prefer to circumvent the Constitution all altogether and find the founding documents archaic instead of timeless.

President Obama's abusive use of the executive order to circumvent Congress thereby infringing on the powers afforded Congress in the Constitution, is just one glaring example of executive over reach and abuse of power. The Constitution impedes his efforts to fundamentally change our great nation so he impudently pushes the envelope a little farther. Obama has only raised the abuse of the executive to a higher level. His predecessors have been aggressively over reaching and abusing the office of the presidency since its inception 200 plus years ago.

Past presidents, and particularly this president, have been "progressing" towards dictatorship in their abuse of executive authority. The use and abuse of executive privilege to circumvent Congress and the judicial branch of our government is impeachable and criminal. If it hasn't been a test case for impeachment, it should be now.

It is no wonder that America is in decline. Our leadership is infected with greed, deception, corruption, narcissism and soaked in socialist dogma. They scoff at the accusation of dictatorship while issuing self-serving decrees. " I am delaying the implementation of this in the Affordable Care Act....I am delaying the cost caps on the Affordable Care Act," picking and choosing which part of a law he likes and disregarding parts of a law he doesn't like. Does he think he is a despot, dictator or monarch? You choose.

Obama's use of the executive order during the campaign to get votes should have been illegal through the violation of campaign law at the very least. But you can't expect a political hack in a corrupted Department of Justice to investigate his own boss. "Never bite the hand that feeds you."

During his re-election campaign, the President used his executive powers and taxpayer's purse to pander to Hispanics regarding border security and illegal immigration issues. He broke the law further by implementing portions of the Dream Act legislation that had been voted down by Congress. He has publicly stated that if he can't work with Congress (if they will not submit he means) then he will use all interpretive legal powers and interpretive legal avenues available to him to get his way. It doesn't mean he has additional powers or avenues, but he is an attorney, so he will create them for himself as needed. He'll be out of office long before the judiciary could ever address the abuse of power issues. He is like a spoiled little boy who takes his ball and runs home when he doesn't get his way.

These abuses are not just prevalent in the Executive Branch. The majorities in both houses of Congress have been bought; their influences purchased and are additionally responsible for accelerating our country's decline. Obamacare and comprehensive illegal immigration reform will seal our coffin. These disasters are clearly on the shoulders of the Congress.

Then there is the issue of sex in America. Novels could and have been written on the act of sex. In fact, you could probably dedicate a whole library to books on sex. I know there is a whole entertainment industry dedicated to sex and then there is the porn industry too! The human being is a unique animal by being basically primal with a conscience. Those without a conscience are known as psychopaths or narcissi. (Let's not go there again.)

Conscience drives our moral compass of right and wrong. Sex has a long and colorful history. It is one physical act that we all share in common. The original settlers from the old countries came to America seeking peace and the ability to practice their faith freely. They had strict laws and rules governing morality that were put in place to maintain order in the community.

Permitted sex was approved between a man and woman in the institution of matrimony. In addition, there were prostitutes, adulterers, saloons and other houses of ill repute where more unsavory acts were performed. Houses of ill repute not very different from our White House when the Kennedy's and Clinton's were living there.

However, unlike today, they were not promoted as normal, acceptable or encouraged behavior. In most, if not all instances, those forms of sex were illegal. Throughout her history, America has had a rather private view of sex. It was a private individual matter between two consenting adults.

The pendulum of sex has swung from the conservative Victorian period, to the promiscuous speak easy days of the Roaring 20's, to the conservative and romantic period of World War II. The birth of Rock N Roll brought with it hip gyrations and "The Summer Knows." The 60's and 70's brought about the complete sexual revolution and free love. All sex, any kind of sex, is acceptable at any place or anytime with anyone you please. Now it appears that there is no pendulum rocking back and forth seeking balance.

Everything is acceptable and it is certainly not individual or private. Prude maybe, but our moral compass seems to have bi-polar disorder to the max. The warp speed advances in technology, a completely immoral and obscene entertainment industry, and a secular society without the moral compass or confines of the church, have made sex and every other moral depravity acceptable and available to all at the touch of a switch or key. America has been very blessed with bountiful treasures, but we seem to abuse these gifts and luxuries which in return accelerate our decline.

The only thing that remains the same and unchanged is that man is basically primal with a conscience. Man is still tempted by the sins inherent to his very existence. Maybe that is why most of us feel guilty when we know we are doing something wrong. If you take away the conscience and any semblance of right and wrong, you lose your moral compass and your soul. Then you have devolved back to nothing more than a primal animal. It seems evident to me that America is on the fast track to moral mediocrity. This too is a major problem for our society.

Other issues that tear at the moral fabric of America include drug abuse, physical and mental addictions, excessive debt and the promotion and acceptance of deviant behavior as normal through multiple forms of mass media. We all are encumbered by the destruction of our rights to privacy and constant government over reach and interference in our everyday lives. Our republic stays in a static and chaotic state.

Our schools are substandard because we keep lowering the bar of achievement for our children. Domestic issues plaguing America such as gang violence, fatherless families, poor education and the slavery created in the inner city plantations continue to hamper real progress. These problems are made worse by government entitlement programs; unconstitutional programs not within their power or purview to provide. Programs by design which waste financial resources retard the economy and severally hinder true progress.

Hopefully, we will be able to address these and other problems that plague America in the following pages. Come on America, we need to have and settle these uncomfortable discussions once and for all in order for America to return to her former glory.

Immigration

Undocumented Alien is PC BS- They are Illegal Aliens and Criminals

I don't care who is in power when it is done, or which party promotes it. Amnesty is not an acceptable alternative for people who break the law. It didn't work in the 1980's and it isn't going to work now either.

The biggest thing that would be accomplished by amnesty is an understanding that if you break the law it is acceptable. It is justification for anarchy; this is not what America stands for.

We are a country of laws instituted for the protection and welfare of all American citizens. The laws we have implemented are not to protect those who have crossed our borders illegally. We need to enforce the existing laws on the books and deport those here illegally. Your compassion is misplaced if you waste it on people who do not accept responsibility for their actions and who have broken the law.

We need to build the actual fence, not a technological fence and secure the border as we were promised by our federal government. We need the federal government to enforce the law. If the federal won't provide the security mandated by the US Constitution, then they shouldn't interfere with the Border States when they attempt to enforce the law.

It is evident that this administration with the backing of the Democrat party has intentionally and effectively circumvented the law through the use of the executive order. Again this should be grounds for impeachment for aiding and abetting our enemies; the constitutional offense of treason. Yes, people who cross our borders illegally are foreign enemies of the United States.

No, it doesn't feel good (sorry for all you overemotional women and androgynous males) or bring any sense of satisfaction to deport illegal aliens or their American children. It is inconvenient and as expensive as hell to deport them. I agree that it is immoral to break up their families, so we should deport their children with them.

If the children are born in America, and thereby determined to be American citizens, they can return with or without their parent when they attain legal age. But in all instances immigrants should come to America legally and through the proper immigration systems in place.

Illegal aliens are a drain on American resources. This is not an attack on Hispanics. If a disproportionate number of illegal aliens are Hispanic that means that there are more illegal aliens that are Hispanic. It is not a racial slight or slur. It is an unfortunate fact.

Illegal aliens use government social and medical services thereby denying access to American citizens and those immigrants who are here legally. In addition, legal Americans and legal immigrants are paying taxes for the services being used and abused by the illegal aliens.

Anchor babies; babies born to illegal aliens in America should not be granted blanket US citizenship. If they are born to Mexicans nationals, they are Mexican. If they are Chinese nationals, they are Chinese. There is no provision in the US Constitution granting US citizenship to the children of foreign nationals in our country. This is a legal misinterpretation of the intent of the Constitution; I do not believe it is settled law. This is a political misinterpretation of the Constitution to increase the Democrat voting base. The US Constitution should, at the very least, be amended to clarify this position. The answer always has been and still should be as per the laws governing such illegal actions-*Deport.*

You will hear the argument that you can't deport 11 or 17 million people (government calculated guestamits). First you would have to locate and then pay to deport them. But look at all the money that you would be saving. You would be saving on government social service and medical costs; think of the savings in Obamacare alone.

You would be saving on court costs and jail costs. You would be recapturing American money that is being shipped to Mexico. The second largest source of revenue for the Mexican government after oil revenue is American money shipped home by legal and illegal aliens.

We will be freeing up domestic and agricultural jobs all over our country. We will provide newly vacated jobs as a hand up to the legal Americans suffering in our inner city plantations. At the same time we will be emptying beds in the inner city which are also providing sanctuaries for illegal aliens.

 Illegal immigrants do not pay taxes. If they did pay taxes it would be easy for the government to round them up and deport them. What money they do secure they send back to their country of origin tax free.

Illegal immigrants drain social services such as Medicaid, welfare, public education and other related benefits which have been confiscated from the tax payers. Even though politicians and political pundits rush to deny the charge, illegal aliens do take jobs away from legal guest workers and American citizens. They do commit violent crimes requiring legal resources and clogging up an already over loaded judiciary. In truth, it is cheaper to deport than to provide asylum, prison space, three squares or other social/welfare benefits provided with taxpayer's money.

Politicians aren't worried about your tax dollars. They want amnesty so they can secure the 11 to 17 million democrat votes; that's it in a nutshell. The party that will benefit the most is the Democrat Party. They will create a new inner city Hispanic victim and buy a new voting base with the taxpayer's money.

There are volumes and volumes of federal, state and local laws currently on the books that need to be enforced. If these laws are not enforced by the Executive Branch or through the Department of Justice, they should be high crimes against the American people. Those responsible for not upholding the laws of the land should be removed from office. There should be impeachment proceeding for dereliction of duty for not protecting the sovereignty of the American people. Doesn't the swearing into political office dictate this and require the promise to protect the American people? Isn't the President supposed to uphold the laws of the land, the US Constitution and the Bill of Rights? Even the ones he doesn't like or agree with?

Treason is a crime that can be charged for aiding and abetting a foreign enemy. Why hasn't this administration and past administrations been impeached for treason? This is a serious American issue and threat to our sovereignty that does not, I repeat, does not need comprehensive reform. It needs the enforcement of existing law.

It is most unfortunate and regrettable that children are going to be collateral damage for the criminal behavior of their parents. This is a travesty that has been practiced through time. This happens every day in this country and around the world. You have to look no further than the viciously murdered inner city kids in Chicago. Kids are abused, molested, sold into slavery, domestically deprived, and poorly educated in our public school system. What does that have to do with them being in this country illegally? Try sneaking into Mexico, Cuba or any country in South America with your children and see what happens when you illegally cross their borders.

Laws should not be affected by feelings or enforced discriminately. They are a form of justice and justice is or should be blind. Tell me about your human rights or American rights when you are thrown into prisons in other third world countries. They don't ask you how you *feel* about your incarceration or make sure you have three square meals. They don't have activist judges letting hardened criminals or illegal aliens out of jail because the little bastards are overcrowded, uncomfortable or completed their minimum sentence requirements regardless of the severity of the crimes they have committed. You may never make it out of those prisons alive more or less be seen or heard from again.

Remember, only the criminals in governments get diplomatic immunity. The rest of us law abiding citizens are held accountable for our actions. Following the strict enforcement of existing laws does not reflect negatively on America. We are a compassionate and caring country and we welcome all who come here legally. In return, we should not reward those who come here illegally.

We can have empathy for the plight of the illegal alien, but two wrongs do not make a right. People need to be responsible for their actions or inactions. The liberals, pacifists and other losers in our society think that you should not be held responsible for your mistakes. It is someone else's fault and you are a victim. The majority of American citizens do not agree.

Our message isn't in line with the leftist propaganda machine that is represented by the tingly leg mainstream media or Socialist Progressive Democrat Party. The majority of Americans believe illegal aliens need to be deported and get in line to return under legal status. Why make it harder or more expensive than it has to be. Oh yeah, I almost forgot. The Democrats need the illegal aliens to keep illegally registering and illegally voting for their socialist party candidates. It would cost socialist progressive a lot less money to secure these votes if they were given legal status through amnesty and we have an election just around the corner.

Illegal Sanctuaries

The church and state are determined to be constitutionally separate in the United States. This is true but only if it doesn't conflict with the political agenda of the Democrats on any given day.

The churches though separate, are still subject to the laws of the land. So are the states, local municipalities and all businesses for that matter. By law, the church does not have the right to harbor illegal aliens and openly disregard the law. They should clothe, feed and tend to their spiritual needs, but then they have to turn them over to the federal government for deportation. This is how our legal system currently works; through laws. I think that is the way it is supposed to work anyway.

There are a few rogue clergy members but there isn't any church doctrine that I am aware of that encourages hiding criminals from law enforcement. It was cute in the Sound of Music, but we need a touch of reality here. If churches do not comply with immigration laws, their tax exempt status as a church should be rescinded and they should be recognized and licensed as a boarding house, motel or hotel.

Once they are properly licensed they should be subject to all taxes, rules and regulations applicable to any other type of hospitality business. This would eliminate the tax exemption status which churches currently enjoy and allow them to harbor illegal aliens until the law enforcement officers get around to enforcing the laws.

States and local municipalities that provide sanctuary to illegal aliens, employ illegal aliens, or have businesses breaking the law by employing illegal aliens should have to pay for their crimes too. States with cities that don't comply with federal immigration laws should have their federal funds withheld until they come into compliance. States should also withhold federal and state funds from sanctuary cities until they come into compliance.

Businesses that openly hire illegal's without the proper documentation should be severely fined or be subject to other legal recourse. However, businesses should not be held responsible if they were deceived or tricked into hiring an illegal alien through forged documentation. It is very common practice for illegal aliens to have counterfeit green cards (temp visas), state identification cards, state driver's licenses, birth certificates, and social security cards. The business that is the victim of this type of fraudulent crime should be exonerated and the two time criminal (committing fraud and being here illegally) should be deported expeditiously.

There is no legal carve out for allowing local communities, cities, states or even the federal government to intentionally and blatantly circumvent the laws of the land. This harbors back to the idea that one is responsible for one's actions. You can't break the law just because you don't like the law. You can't choose to ignore enforcement of the law, when you have sworn an oath to uphold the law. You can't claim federal law trumping state law and then not enforce the federal law and further encumber the law enforcement officers of the individual states from protecting their borders. But this is exactly what is happening in America. Until such time as we deport and enforce existing law, the border crisis will continue.

Americans Should never allow anything in Washington DC to be "Comprehensive"

About 12 years ago there was a universal call for comprehensive immigration reform. Of course it was only universal in Washington D.C.'s universe, the leftist universe and the liberal media. It was pretty much a joke, like the creation of the national police force known as the Department of Homeland Security to the other 300 million Americans across the country.

The government was going to make another attempt do something comprehensively. Ideas of amnesty, deportation, paths to citizenships and a whole myriad of "brilliant think tank" ideas were floated around Washington DC. Tanks and things floating in them always remind me of Washington DC as do most cesspools. You usually get a big pile of comprehensive crap like Obamacare.

This proposal during the Bush administration for "comprehensive immigration reform," was no different except thankfully it didn't come to pass. When the great leaders of Washington presented their ideas to the public, the public said a definitive "NO" to the comprehensive concept. Rest assured though that patience is a virtue, and the socialists are definitely patient but are incapable of pulling off virtuous. Now we are faced with yet another attempt at amnesty through a bipartisan (a term equivalent to turncoat or traitor) "comprehensive immigration plan." Say goodbye now Rubio. We had high hopes for that boy.

The American people told the lawmakers to first stop the hemorrhaging at the border by building a fence. Our illustrious leaders agreed to build the fence. As of this writing, the fence has not been completed and many of those same leaders have lost their luster. Coyotes and their human cargo continue to pass freely over the borders of Texas, Arizona, New Mexico and California carrying illegal drugs and other contraband with little or no legal consequence. These illegal border crossings are being encouraged by this President and the political hacks appointed by him in law enforcement and many leftists in Congress.

Nice term-Comprehensive. It gives the impression of one complete fix to all problems. The only thing is that problems are fluid and never comprehensively corrected. I am a firm believer in the KISS principle- Keep It Simple Stupid; thus build the fence.

An example of the KISS principle is this: it is illegal to kill a person. Abortion is murder and therefore illegal.
You can call the baby a mass of cells. You can claim a woman's right to her body. You can pretty much and most have, come to the conclusion that abortion is ok. It covers up the crime of gender approved murder and a shit load of guilt that accompanies it if everybody thinks it is ok. However, it is the murder of a person; simple concept and simple reality. It doesn't take a genius to say it nor one to understand it. I can assure you I am no genius.

Every time the government tries to do things comprehensively, they screw it up. Look at the atrocities that government has created under comprehensive dogma. You have the Department Human Health Services which oversee the implementation and rulemaking for comprehensive medical nightmare Obamacare. The collective of elected idiots, including the President and Congress, didn't even read the damn bill.

It doesn't say much for the electorate who voted for these supposedly "brilliant" leaders either. Other comprehensive tragedies inflicted on the American people by an inept federal government are the EPA, NSA, IRS, Social Security, Medicaid and Medicare; countless others, far too many to list here. You have hundreds of thousands of government employees creating tons of programs and regulations to comprehensively fix every possible ailment known to man. They successfully and comprehensively create more problems than they fix.

Illegal immigration is one such problem that does not need to be corrected or addressed through comprehensive legislation. Build the fence, protect the borders, deport the illegal aliens, and grant return visas if they are determined to be American citizens when they attain legal age. Pathways to obtain visas and attain citizenship are already available in the United States. Just build the fence and secure the borders already!

As of today, the Federal government, this administration in particular, still hasn't built the fence, but they have succeeded in "comprehensively" destroying the housing market, banking industry and the best healthcare system the world has ever known in $1/12^{th}$ the time.

They were also comprehensively responsible for killing American border agents with failed crime prevention programs like "Fast and Furious" in addition to the four dead Americans in Benghazi. You can thank the Obama administration, Hillary Clinton and the far left Democrats for no fence. You can additionally thank them for creating enormous debt, excessive deficit spending and all the other travesties aforementioned.

Then there is the environmentalist dream child, the Department of Environmental Protection. Another comprehensive plan put into place to address America's energy resources. This department was created with the best of intentions by our politicians to appease the environmentalists of the Sierra Club, Green Peace, Audubon and whatever remains of the Woodstock crowd. Oh yeah, they are the degenerate professors from the 60's enjoying tenure at our most prestigious' universities.

The Congress heeded the call of the wild who wanted to protect our air, ozone, drinking water and waterways with the creation of this massive department. However, over time it reached its pinnacle of success by morphing into an over reaching regulatory agency that regulates the carbon dioxide you exhale. Yes, it is true. You need to apply for a carbon credit to breathe! Was that the comprehensive intent of this agency? No! Is it a typical result of comprehensive governance from Washington DC? You betcha!

The EPA, like most agencies in the federal government, does provide a convenient whipping boy for Congress. Congress will place blame on the EPA when some new crisis occurs like an oil spill or when the public gets wind of proposed carbon credit fees and taxes for exhaling. These problems are always sent to Congressional committees where the news cameras can capture the circus of House or Senate members grandstanding for the public.

You know the Congress wasn't responsible for that spill. It was inadequate regulations, rules and enforcement by the EPA. If the agency would have had more regulations, then the spill wouldn't have occurred. "Heads are going to roll." *Yada! Yada! Yada!*

In actuality, I've never seen any blood flow from these hearings and in three days everything will be swept under the rug. But rest assured the EPA miscreant's will be working diligently to create more rules and regulations to stop future spills.

The most inept federal employees are promoted and shuffled to new government union protected jobs and nothing ever changes. Except guarantees of new regulations and further abuse of comprehensive power. Even the elected officials seem to stay forever until their tan skin matches the leather thrones that they have purchased for themselves through our US Treasury.

There are a multitude of other agencies and other abuses. These special agencies are in state and local governments too. They are all the result of comprehensively addressing a problem or group of problems as perceived by government. They may not even be real but you know what they say about perception being reality.

The federal government does a great disservice to us all when they create massive bureaucracies to implement regulations and rules to remedy our nation's ills. They comprehensively infringe upon our constitutional rights and protections while creating substantially more problems than they solve.

If you can take away one thing from this chapter, take this as gospel. Even you atheist who can't stomach to read the gospel should learn this fact. When the government says "comprehensive" nothing positive will come out of it. Again I point to the fence, Dodd/Frank personally and legislatively, Fannie Mae, Freddie Mac, the Department of Homeland Security(or Obama's SS as I like to call it), General Motors, and the mother of all comprehensive plans, Obamacare.

Yes, destruction of the best healthcare system in the world and forced servitude for all! Those who work are the ones who I really meant to address here; not the 55% who represent the moocher class. They're so thoroughly entrenched in ignorance, they have no idea they have already been enslaved.

ILLEGAL ALIENS are titled illegal aliens for a reason. They are here illegally and are aliens on our shores. This is not rocket science. "Undocumented persons" is a liberal progressive switch of hand so that we don't ostracize those criminals who came here illegally seeking a better life at your expense.

The same reason the liberals changed the government food welfare program from food stamps to SNAP. The same reason liberals use EBT cards instead of actual food coupons. They don't want moochers stigmatized for accepting state handouts. They need people dependent and to use these handouts. The next politically correct progressive expression will be "undocumented citizen of the world." You can watch its birth when as it becomes a standard form of speech in the Democrat Party's Solidarity playbook.

The Democrat Party and this administration have been very successful in dividing this nation by class, gender and through race warfare. The Democrat Party has the legitimate Latin community thinking that being here illegally is acceptable and that dissent is racially motivated. The far left in the Democrat party are encouraging the Hispanic community to join the ever growing class of victims they have created in America. They are making room to house them and take care of all their needs in their inner city plantations. Pathetic!

We Don't need More Laws, We need More Law Enforcement

It does not take massive legislation or a bunch of special interest lobbyists to correct the immigration problem in the United States. We definitely don't need a corrupt third world government like Mexico or a conglomerate of third world Islamic countries like those housed in the UN, dictating our immigration policy.

These shady third world governments benefit when our money is shipped over the border to their drug cartels and their indigent populations. We pay the most UN costs, more than any other member nation in the organization and we are constantly getting berated by its leeching membership.

In order to address and stem the tide of illegal immigration in this country, three things have to occur.

> 1) The existing federal laws on the books need to be enforced.
> 2) People here illegally need to be deported.
> 3) Build the fence.

The reason the American people do not trust the federal government is because we have played this game before with the same results. Nothing was done that was promised.

Ronald Reagan instituted an amnesty program in the 1980's. It was intended to be a bipartisan attempt to begin to correct the illegal alien problem. It was a very compassionate approach to a costly and festering problem.

It was thought that the legislators in both houses would come together, compromise and fix the overall problem through *comprehensive legislation*. Of course, like all things comprehensive in Washington, only the easy amnesty part was comprehensively completed.

It's amusing to see the Democrats take credit for that amnesty decision instituted by Ronald Reagan when it's time to grovel and pander on the campaign trail for the Latino vote today. Democrats are always taking credit for positive legislation when they were usually on the opposing side of the issues. But the moral of the story here is that the hard parts of comprehensive reforms or the other half of a compromise never gets completed in Washington DC.

One thing is absolutely true though in Washington. The Democrats are famous for not holding up their end of any compromise or bargain. We just saw this play out in the Fiscal Cliff debacle in December 2012. Democrats are the first too scream for compromise, and Republicans always concede. Each time the Republicans get stabbed in the back, look like played fools and the Democrats don't fulfill their commitments to the American people and still come out smelling like roses. Remember though, the rose stem is full of pricks.

Recently the U.S. Senate, the majority being Democrats, and President Obama pushed and succeeded in raising taxes on the American people. These funds were necessary to buy more votes through expanding entitlement moocher programs such as unemployment benefits and disability payments; but that's another story.

 The Democrats got the taxes requested through "compromise" but they didn't cut any spending as they agreed to in the "compromise." In fact, the Democrats have accelerated entitlement spending increasing our national debt to 17 trillion dollars.

The political class prostitutes themselves to all classes in our country. That is how politicians secure votes necessary to maintain power. They need the illegal aliens to stay and vote them into office. Legal or illegal is of no consequence to liberal socialist posing as Progressive Democrats in America.

This is why illegal aliens receive food stamps and other tax payer social services like Medicaid. This is why politicians, local, state and federal, the majority being Democrats, their political arm the national news media and unions pander to the poor and ignorant in our society. The permanent poor secure their election and maintain their politburo power and control over the government and thereby the people.

There is no need for new laws. There are adequate laws on the books to handle our border situations. The problem is that crooked far left politicians interfere with law enforcement agencies duties by directly ordering officers not to enforce the laws.

These laws are the same laws they have sworn to uphold in the US Constitution. It appears this Administration and its Department of Justice are not subject to the laws of the land. Despots rarely abide by the laws and in fact, pervert the intent of the laws to serve their purpose. This is called brilliance in today's political circles, by our press, the collegiate elite or anyone in the Regressive Party. You pick.

There could be impeachable grounds here if the legislative branch had not allowed itself to become so inconsequential. The Senate and House are getting played by the President. They convene a multitude of committees grandstanding for the media's benefit with no justice for the dead from Fast and Furious to the dead Americans in Benghazi. There are many laws that have been broken and no one in political office is being held accountable. The Senate and the House are not the only ones being played by this President; so are the American people.

As long as it is for the good of the politburo party over the good of the country, America will continue to decline. The borders will remain porous because it is in the political class's best interest to allow the fluid movement of illegal aliens across our borders. These corrupted political leaders have weaseled their way into state and local positions too.

Many one-world- order types, the Democratic Party, foreign socialists, Ivy League professors, and legal scholars do not believe in our country's sovereign rights, our states sovereign rights or the establishment of borders. They believe in one world with no borders and world citizenship. Now isn't that refreshingly progressive?!

They believe resources of the world should be "redistributed" to those according to their needs. They believe, like our President and his court of circus clowns, that the treasures of the United States need to be "redistributed" to the rest of the world. Our sacrilege is that we have been blessed with an abundance of resources which we do not deserve. We are not entitled to these resources as per edict of this President and the radical left in the Democrat Party.

Obama Sr. was a communist who believed such none sense. He was against colonialism and capitalism. Of course, you would expect him to think like this. He was the product of a third world colonial country and a bit of a hypocrite. He enjoyed the benefits of American life, an Ivy League education, wine, women and song, all the while condemning the very foundation of our country. I believe this belief system has been successfully passed down to his son. Laws must be circumvented or intentionally broken if necessary in order to achieve these far left goals. These laws may get in the way of our fundamental transformation. Therefore, we will just go around them!

What's with the Fence?

After 9/11, America came together for one very brief moment. The smoke hadn't cleared before the tragedy of that day was turned into a national travesty. People wanted to know how such an attack could be accomplished on American soil.

American society could not understand the hatred shown against her by the Islamist fanatics from the Middle East. After all we provide more money and aid to the Middle East and Africa than any other country in the world. We have the largest and greatest military and have encourage democracy and world peace through military strength. We promote freedom and liberty throughout the world. How could this happen to us? We are the nice guys. Right?!

The American people have squandered trillions of dollars in taxes and treasures to these foreign countries while constantly being attacked by the beneficiaries of our benevolence. President Bush stepped up providing leadership, calm and compassion. For just a moment it was the American people over politics.

There were other things we just couldn't understand. We had the FBI, CIA, NSA, Interpol and a slew of other covert operations all over the world. Even the President wanted to know how this attack could happen and what the nation needed to do to prevent it in the future. The typical political response was knee jerk, over emotional and you guessed it- comprehensive.

President Bush started his campaign with the help of an enthusiastic nanny-state legislature to create comprehensive ways to make sure this type of attack never happened again. He created the largest travesty (after the Fed Reserve and the EPA) ever to be inflicted upon the American people. He started the Department of Homeland Security, a national police force.

He worked with Congress to chip away at our privacy and freedoms with the institution of the Patriot Act. We graciously and willingly gave up some of our privacy and liberty for the sake of the national interest. We never imagined at that time, that relinquishing some of our rights would be abused as egregiously as they have been recently by our government.

The DHS is a department which has been given far reaching power which allows it to disregard every individual right guaranteed every American citizen by the US Constitution. This may not have been the intent of the department but it is definitely a dire consequence of the department's development and "evolution." The Department of Homeland Security has more power than all the other federal law enforcement agencies created before it. It even has unlimited powers over those agencies.

The disappointing fact is that the authority it exercises is under control of the Executive Branch and not the Legislative branch. It is much easier to corrupt one than many; the action's of this administration affirms this point. This excessive concentration of power in the Executive Branch is a very dangerous and potentially detrimental to the balance of power in American government. This is eerily reminiscent of another time in history when a maniacal dictator rose with his national police force in Germany.

To further complicate matters, we have a complicit press that acts as the fourth branch of government that should be known as the Department of Propaganda; a press corps that would make Woodrow Wilson, Hitler, Lenin, Chavez and Anita Dunn proud. This is a press that is supposed to be the last line of defense for the American people against an overbearing, shady and tyrannical government. Our press is supposed to be the final protector of the people by exposing political deceit and corruption committed by those in public office. The American press today is failing the American people by not investigating, demanding answers and reporting on the crimes being committed against us.

Often times they will not report on crimes that they feel has been perpetrated by an unfortunate victim of an oppressive society. These crimes would be committed by illegal aliens, black on white crime or black on black crime. They don't report and everything remains status quo. They are failing the American people by not finding out who is stopping the laws from being enforced in this country. They are derelict in their duties when they intentionally don't report information on who is responsible for lax border security, lax law enforcement, the death of American border agents and why the fence promised hasn't been completed.

The Department of Homeland Security is the first national police force in the United States and this police force is under the direct authority of the President of the United States. It is not a national or foreign spy agency like the CIA or NSA. It is not an agency to enforce federal laws broken across state lines like the FBI. It is not an arm of the military. It is a public police force over the American people with sweeping powers over all enforcement and clandestine agencies in the United States.

Hitler, Stalin and Mao all empowered substantial national police forces. The DHS is no different. Can you see where these powers could potentially be abused and go wrong under the leadership of a socialist Administration. Unchecked power corrupts completely.

The Department of Homeland Security under the Obama administration has been used to stop immigration laws from being enforced in the United State. They have stopped or restricted deportations. This has been accomplished through the abuse of the executive order or internally by policies and guidelines instituted by Janet Napolitano and DHS staff. The President and DHS have interfered with ICE and the ATF in the execution of their legal duties.

They have ordered these agencies to stop the enforcement of existing law related to illegal immigration. The President and DHS should have had knowledge or been privy to information from the Department of Justice regarding the use of special op forces for illegal programs such as Fast and Furious. I believe the President and DHS were fully aware of the program and other programs put into operation by the Department of Justice. A failed program which came at a cost of American lives and treasure for which no one has been brought to justice.

There has recently been a legal battle between the law enforcement agency ICE and the Administration. ICE is suing the Federal Government for not allowing them to enforce the immigration laws they have been sworn to uphold. It probably won't be reported extensively in the press.

When the Executive Branch of the Government isn't interfering in enforcement of immigration law, either through the Department of Homeland Security or Department of Faux Justice, then the judicial activist on the bench start releasing these criminal aliens back onto the streets.

This is not just the executive and the judiciary skirting the law, you have whole cities and states thumbing their noses at the federal laws already on the books. Why should they follow the law when there are no consequences for their actions? Why should states enforce federal laws when the federal government doesn't enforce their laws? This is the same thing that criminals and residents of the inner city plantations learn. There are no consequences for your actions and you are not held responsible for your actions.

President Obama has attacked border states like Arizona from his executive perch. He has been eager and with accommodating group of his lap dogs at the press, able to broadcast his message effectively to the ignorant masses. He verbally attacked Arizona's governor Jan Brewer for enforcing the laws he was elected and bound by the US Constitution to enforce. Finally, he ended up calling his hounds at the DOJ to harass and file suit against Arizona and her sovereign right to protect her borders.

Obama's Department of Justice filed suit against Arizona, a sovereign state, when they were legislating state law in order to protect their borders. Then the President used his bully pulpit and his surrogates, Janet Napolitano at DHS and Eric Holder at the DOJ, to belittle the Governor for trying to protect her citizens when the feds would not do so.

You see it is not the need for more laws. It is the need for competent leadership which is sorely lacking in this President, his administration and in his party. It is the need for enforcement of existing laws. It is the need for elected leaders to uphold their oaths of office and enforce the laws already on the books. This would eliminate the need for any more comprehensive disasters from Washington.

In closing, the last piece of immigration reform we authorized and demanded as the American people, was to build a fence along the southern US border. If I am not mistaken this President, his Democrat/Socialists cohorts in the Legislature and the head of his national police force at DHS, have stopped building the fence.

The Democrats had absolute power for two years and majority power for five years. The fence has not been completed to date. Do you think you're better protected now than 9/11? Think again and let me know when you see the completed fence in place!

Education in America

Dummying Down of America – Who teaches the Teachers?

America's education system is and has been in major decline. This decline started the day public education was introduced but accelerated to warp speed in the 1960's. It has "progressed" through the primary, secondary and college level education over time to the mess we currently operating today. We are no longer teaching mathematics, science, reading and writing in primary and secondary education. We are however providing expensive day care, nursery facilities and meal plans with the taxpayer's education dollars. Don't get me wrong. We literally throw billions of dollars at education in this country and haven't seen much bang for the buck as a result. The decline can't be blamed on a lack of funds.

We have financed a bunch of feel good socialist programs but a quality education; not so much. We have earth day, bully free day, bring both dads' to school day and the ever popular and progressive gender bending and diversity training courses.

It seems only logical that public schools would be turned into government restaurants. Food service is one of those social programs that the federal government seems to excel in. What do you expect when 40 million people are on food stamps? Just make sure that you use Michelle's Food Pyramid or you will not receive those valuable federal education dollars.

The elitist and professional educators who preach the utopian vision of total equality live in an unrealistic dream world. There can never be equality. We need to return to our biology books and think animal kingdom and survival of the fittest. The so-called professionally educated elites would be the first to parish from the food chain left to their own demise.

The fact that they dwell in houses of socialist theory, our universities, does not inherently make them the best teachers or necessarily the best leaders. Don't misunderstand me. We have some outstanding universities that immerse their students in extremely important subjects such as physics, engineering and medicine. However, there are many colleges and universities that simply cater to liberal philosophy and theory.

In my opinion, some of the easiest and least useful of all college classes are in the liberal arts. There are liberal classes that teach political science, immersing the students in socialist thought for example. These classes are required study. They serve as pre-requisites needed to proceed to other required courses when seeking a liberal art degree. The student has no choice in the matter if he/she is seeking a liberal arts degree. These are the same colleges that produce many of our primary and secondary educators. This is the starting point for the liberal indoctrination of our citizenry.

It is here where political and social theory is taught and where liberal brainwashing begins. There are liberal art and science colleges. However, I am speaking only of liberal art curriculums that teach political and social theory. Other classes that fit appropriately and comfortably into these categories are political science, sociology, environmental studies, and eastern religions.

It would seem with all the billions of dollars poured into higher education through endowments, government grants and other tax incentives, a better system of lifting the poor out of poverty would have surfaced from our universities and found its way into our public school systems; but it hasn't. It appears these brilliant professors are not the exceptional scholars they self- proclaim to be.

As long as man is imperfect, so shall be his world. Therefore, there will be no perfect utopian societies because there is no perfect man. If a professor teaches that such perfection is attainable, it would be rubbish. But that is exactly what liberal theory alludes to; attainable perfection. The closest thing to a perfect society was the founding of America and the creation of her core documents; the US Constitution and Bill of Rights. Many in the liberal arts field teach that America is an oppressive and greedy society and that socialism or even communism is a better alternative.

Our republic/capitalist based system allows for individual exceptionalism and personal achievement. This system of governance acknowledges the fact that we are not all equal but we are all afforded opportunities to reach our maximum potential as human beings. Our timeless founding documents protect the individual's autonomy and guarantee him his rights of life, liberty and the pursuit of happiness. There is no socialist constitution that presents the opportunity for one to reach one's individual perfection.

A number of professors and far left members in the Democrat Party teach the destruction and demise of our country through subversion and revolution. They encourage class warfare through affirmative action, social promotion, title IX regulations, tenure and numerous other divisive measures. They promote the hiring and retention of liberals into professorships while actively discouraging the hiring or promotion of conservative professors. These are the same professors that teach our children the benefits of utopian socialist theory and sameness; how ironic.

In the past, some of these academic elitists promoted Eugenics, which never seems to be a headline in the history books or discussed in academic social circles. Such acknowledgments would reflect poorly on the liberal professors who wander the halls of our best universities.

You don't need to look hard to find exceptionally bright educators who are enlightening our young men and women today. You have home grown terrorists Bill Ayers and his lovely terrorist wife; both confessed but not convicted murderers, administering their poison to some of America's finest young minds.

You can't forget the extraordinaire anti-capitalist and decrepit old communist flag bearer Francis Fox-Pivens, and the even more incredible American Indian, Chief Ward Churchill. In fact, the weirder, deviant, degenerative and outside the mainstream of America you are, the easier it is to attain tenure and a chair position at our most prestigious universities or have a place in the Obama administration. The more outlandish their liberal theories, the more money they absorb out of each tuition dollar.

Colleges do not teach classes required only for a specific degree. In order to make a better rounded person before they graduate, it has been determined by liberals in academia that a group of undergraduate core studies should be required. This requirement means that all students must take liberal art classes before they can take practical classes which may in fact, pertain to their majors.

Some other examples of liberal art classes would be in areas such as classical music, humanities and theatre. I am sure that a student studying to become a world class physicist would greatly excel in his field if he was required to study Steinbeck, Frost, Eastern Religions or the Supremacy of Socialism. This requirement to take liberal art classes is great for the liberal arts professors. Otherwise no one would spend the tuition dollars on liberal art classes; except for future teachers who are required to take these courses. Colleges teach the teachers liberal thought and the teachers spread their lessons to our youth.

If we eliminated mandatory liberal art classes that teach and promote social and political theory, you would kill three birds with one stone. You would get rid of unnecessary liberal professors that espouse socialist and communist principle but who condemn the American system. You would actually teach classes of importance such as biology, business, law, medicine, engineering, and physics. Last but not least, you would weed out a large number of students who have no business attending college in the first place because the curriculums of advanced study would be too difficult to pass.

We would have the choice to invest our tuition dollars in various studies that might be more conducive to lifting America to her prior prominence in the world. Liberals on College Boards, often professors, have proposed that requiring these liberal art classes makes for a better rounded individual and therefore have mandated them into required study for all degrees. A person can seek enlightenment and rounding when he has a job or during his free time. It can be an extracurricular activity.

I don't have a problem with the arts in general. They should be available if a student wants to take them. However, in my opinion, many liberal art classes that are required do not help students excel in his or her chosen field of advanced study. The requirement of courses in liberal arts imposed on undergraduates unrelated to one's field of study seems completely unnecessary.

Political science classes, interpretations of American history, and other liberal classes provide an opportunity to indoctrinate students, future graduates and teachers in liberal thought and ideology. In order to pass the class you have to have learned their theory and lesson. You don't necessarily have to believe it. But many young people are impressionable and do believe it. This is especially true when there is no counter point on which to balance one's opinion. After you graduate, you will pass what you have learned on to others. Colleges are the starting point for the induction into socialist political thought and it has been effectively indoctrinated into our children and our future teachers.

Requiring someone to take certain liberal arts as a requirement for a degree is a misdirection of education dollars. If a medical student were able to take additional courses in science such as chemistry or physics, they might become a better doctor. A student may stumble upon a cure for cancer in a biology lab; it works in India and China.

India and China are presently moving ahead of us academically in most, if not all fields of math and science. They are succeeding at our expense and it is due to our failing education systems. This failure starts in our colleges because that is who turns out the teachers and the teaching programs. Due to America's public education crisis which has been festering over time, the new American students entering college are insufficiently prepared to be in college; often times requiring the implementation of remedial training.

The 1950's and 1960's ushered in the birth of the suburbs. It was the demise of the extended family and the creation of the nuclear family. Air travel, railroads, and automobile highways allowed Americans to move out of the city. It allowed children to move far away from their parents. These were the decades when the extended family began to disintegrate and the birth of individualism became chic' and promoted on college campuses. It was not proactive and community minded individualism embedded in American exceptionalism, but the "selfish it's all about me" type of individualism taught in liberal circles.

Historically, colleges in America were only accessible to the wealthy or intellectually exceptional people in American Society. The Ivy League school system was created to accommodate the education of this elite class. Many colleges today still provide outstanding educational opportunities but they have opened their doors to a more diverse student body. In many cases, they lowered their admission and curriculum standards to accommodate this new pc imposed diversity.

The accumulation of wealth and the vibrant growth in America's economy post WWII, opened new opportunities for the average Americans to attend college. Since then it has become an American family expectation, if not a misperceived right, for our children to attend college. I have severe reservations regarding the value of these expectations.

We no longer apprentice in trades that service everyday life. We are under the assumption that all children are college material or that it is the next stage of development; what I like to call extended childhood. They are not children but young adults.

We place an unnecessary burden on the academically challenged with our unrealistic expectations that everyone is college material. This is another story for another time. The point here is that colleges have exposed our young men and women to the theory of socialism and have presented it as a viable and superior alternative to the American capitalist system.

Professors teach socialist theory which promises some utopia that doesn't exist and can't be achieved. This utopia can't exist because man is imperfect and we will never be equal. In the classroom they still teach how there is a better political and economic system than what we have here in America. They point to a western European model as an example to prove this theory. They neglect to teach their students that those quasi-socialist governments are crumbling and failing.

The colleges of the 1960's were liberal theaters of free love and self-empowerment. How those social mores fits into the college curriculums then or now is a mystery to me. During this decade the liberal elites started to gain ground in promoting their liberal philosophies. Let's face it; sex, drugs and rock n roll are fun.

The cost of this liberation has been staggering. The liberal schools of higher learning have secured the decline in public education through their beliefs and teachings. The dismantling of the extended family, the increase in the number of poor and the basic moral degradation of the American populace can be placed squarely on the shoulders of academia in America.

Our education system was the best in the world when it catered to the capitalist system and promoted American ingenuity and exceptionalism. America was a country of achievement and a place where all had an opportunity to excel. Everyone wasn't college material back then and they aren't now.

College was an institution of higher learning for the exceptional intellects in our society. It was never meant to be an extension of childhood, a childcare center to teach adulthood to our children. Those lessons were to be learned at home. Our education system wasn't founded on the principle of lowered standards or teaching to the mean. Colleges couldn't grow and profit without self promotion. They depend on private and public funds to stay in operation and pay for those big compensation packages provided to their professors. Colleges would teach you to believe that the only true path to a better life in America is through a college education. It is a fallacy.

There are many great Americans who never attended college and became successful entrepreneurs. The lie is that you need a college degree to be successful in America. That is totally not true. Just by being in America, you are afforded opportunities like nowhere else in the world. You can be an automobile mechanic, captain of a yacht, work in agriculture, become a great chef, or retail executive. You can be dedicated and work hard for a company and climb the corporate ladder.

These are all honorable professions which provide real services and benefits to American life. How often do you call a museum curator in your life or a violinist? Is a college degree even necessary in many occupations?

We are in decline because the publicly educated, let's be honest, the mean educated and socially promoted student is going into college but can't compete or excel in a difficult college curriculum. He or she can't even read at college level. Therefore the colleges lower their standards to keep the tuition dollars flowing. Many university curriculums are water downed, even remedial to some extent.

Foreign students often fill seats in some of our most prestigious university classrooms. In most cases they are academically superior to American students. The best schools have the highest tuitions and the highest ranked students. The excessive tuition costs and higher academic standards required to be the best in many fields of study leaves many exceptional American students out of the running. Is this educational progress? Is this a by-product of a poor public education system in America?

Some degrees will not advance your career or your financial position one bit. This of course is not true if you are employed through the government, protected by union membership and paid with tax dollars. You can work in the field of Pornography (National Endowment of the Arts), Political Science (the study of greed, power, theft, deception and all the virtues inherent to political office), Law (ditto) and Environmental Science (EPA) as a proponent of manmade Global Warming and carbon credit taxation for breathing.

The four years apprenticing in the field you choose to pursue in life would have provided you more stability, experience and increased earnings potential than you would achieve through taking liberal art classes. College should be the exception not the rule in a country so rich in alternative opportunities for advancement.

Everyone is not cut out for college. By pushing the mediocre students to college, we are doing the same thing that they do in public schools. We are lowering our standards and bringing the exceptional down to the mediocre level. College is no longer an institution of higher learning. It is simply an extension of American childhood through remedial education. The unfortunate result of our liberally based college education is the creation of many inadequately trained teachers administering socialist programs instead of teaching core academic courses to our children.

Primary and Secondary Education

The socialist state's purpose and survival is dependent on being responsible for your care from cradle to grave. They must completely control your very existence. What better place to start than by indoctrinating your children's minds in publicly funded schools? The state, through the use of primary and secondary education, is aggressively supplanting the values and morals of the parents, with lower expectations and controlled thought.

Black and white solutions are diametrically opposed to the self interest of the nanny state. Finite solutions to problems do not allow for liberal programs such as diversity training, affirmative action, reverse discrimination and social indoctrination. Therefore we can't have finite solutions.

This type of logic is only endorsed in the pages of the socialist handbook. It has never worked in practice. If it doesn't pertain to promoting divisive class warfare, acceptance of deviant behavior as normal, or race baiting, you won't find it in the index of the Democrat Party playbook.

America's parents have given up their parental rights and responsibilities for raising their children. Knowingly or not, parents have provided a prime opportunity for the government to displace their parental roles and responsibilities through public school system.

Government is always ready and willing to step in and take over when anyone relinquishes their responsibilities. It gives them more control over you and your children. Control means limitless power.

In order to keep up with the "Van Jones'", the progressive ideologies such as self-gratification, self-fulfillment, or quite simply selfishness, have caused both parents to shrug their primary responsibilities of being parents. Sadly and to the detriment of their children, and society at large, many children are being raised in a single parent household. This is definitely the case in the fatherless inner city plantation households.

With one parent absent, or both parents absent, it has been convenient for the state to step in and accept the responsibility for your children and for "your" good. This would never have happened to the American extended families prior to the 1960's. The extended family was the core of American progress. Parents were not willing or able to shirk their responsibilities. Government bailouts weren't an option then and they weren't expected to be. But the 1960's were the start of something far different.

This new liberal progressive "me" era introduced the idea of individual uniqueness. This progressive idea ushered in the birth of the "total acceptance" movement. It encouraged and coddled all forms of deviant and often time's degenerate behavior with the uncompromising or in many cases, coerced need to understand diversity.

The breakdown of the American family and these new classes of victims allowed the regressive democrat party to divide, infiltrate and indoctrinate our children through the public education system. You can see the success of their endeavors by the shear multitude of failures produced by our public schools across the nation today.

Curriculums of reading, writing, arithmetic, physical education, the sciences, and civics were replaced or modified to reach a more "diverse and inclusive" audience. Diverse and inclusive here suggests that we do not teach to the mean, we teach to below the mean. God forbid you work to raise somebody up when it takes half the effort but double the costs to drag them down.

In public high school, the general curriculums taught in the 1970's were Algebra I, Algebra II, Trigonometry, Pre-Calculus and Calculus. Now we teach remedial math 1, 2, 3 and an elective in Social Justice.

Leaves one to wonder, if we are teaching general arithmetic in high school, what are these outstanding public educators teaching in elementary school? This thought is pretty scary but is evidenced by America's continued decline in all areas of core academics.

 We need to make the curriculums more difficult and more demanding. We need to challenge our children. Parents, not the state, need to make children stay in school until they graduate. We need to impress on our children this is their job. This is what is expected of them. This is their responsibility to themselves and to their families. This is their pathway to success.

If they are not attending regular school then they need to be put in alternative schools for the full school day and be taught a trade. It should not be an option and it should be a criminal offense if they don't attend classes. It should be an inconvenience for the parent of the child who isn't attending classes too. Parents, not the government, should be responsible for disciplining and raising their children.

After all, if someone is held responsible for the decisions they make, they don't tend to make the same mistake twice. Of course, if you are a senior in high school and still in general math 1, you have a greater potential to be a proud supporter and beneficiary of the Democrat Party largess.

There will always be rich and poor. What the Obama administration and the public school system are succeeding in doing is destroying America's middle class. The elitist class, inclusive of professional educators, politicians, media moguls and all those who promote the concept of total equality are doing our youth a great disserve.

They live in an unrealistic dream world. They need to get out of the classroom and live in the real world where they may actually have to produce something of value. Teachers promote socialist doctrine through the implementation of social programs and menial academic curriculums. In essence, they test these statist theories on our children using them as lab rats. Remember the number 1 musical hit-MMM Obama being sung by the "public" school children; another prime example of public education in practice.

These educators and their supporters are committing the most egregious of sins. They are not just exposing but suffocating our children in the dogma of socialism. I do not feel I have to list the litany of programs forced by the federal and state governments into the public school system to prove my point. These government mandated liberal programs take valuable resources and teaching time away from more important areas of study. They are the equivalent of academic cancers infecting our classrooms.

Public schools must be important to American society because we keep throwing billions and ever increasing billions of dollars at them. We are still receiving the same pathetic results with little or no improvement. This does not reflect well on the American university system, the public education system or us as Americans who don't demand a better return on our investment. Maybe we are getting the return we deserve.

If the importance of an education isn't important enough to treat its disregard as a crime, then you can blame the liberals in our society and the parents of these juvenile delinquents for the crimes they will commit after they drop out.

Schools should concentrate on raising the academic standards of American education. Social services should not be provided in the school environment. Social services if administered at all should be at the local level, not at the national level. The food programs should be eliminated. If a girl has a baby, the school does not need to provide daycare. The pregnant girl and the child's father, when determined, should be sent to an alternative school.

The federal Head Start program is a $200 billion dollar government boondoggle and should be eliminated. The No Child Left Behind is an oxymoron when that is exactly what happens when the program is federally administered. This is another example of government supplanting the roles and responsibilities of the parents.

Children need to learn early that there is a consequence for their actions and inactions. Yes, it is unfortunate that you didn't practice safe sex, or that you were having sex that you weren't prepared for in the first place. But shit happens, it's your fault, and we still love you but...case closed, now close your legs and move on!

We need to raise our expectations for academic excellence to its highest level. We owe it to our children to teach them reading, writing, arithmetic, the sciences and American civics in primary and secondary schools. We need to teach our children about the best form of government; the American democratic republic. We need to teach them about the best economic system in the world- American capitalism. Those are classes designed around true progress and achievement which should be the minimums mandated in all public schools if we are going to continue to fund public education. In all cases, public education should be funded locally and not through the federal government. We need to decentralize federal power and control.

We need our children to seek success and personal fulfillment through hard work. This can't be accomplished in a corrupted public education system planned by the federal government, run by unions and drenched in statist socialist drivel. This can't be accomplished when we teach to the mean instead of to ones individual potential.

We need to abolish all traces of socialism, communism, and fascism in our public education system before it is too late. My fear is that it is too late and the tentacles of mediocrity are already firmly planted in our public education system.

Unions Negative Influence on Education

There is another reason even beyond the currently watered downed curriculums which is responsible for our children's academic decline. It is the Public School Unions; teachers, administrators, janitors, cafeteria workers and crossing guards. Not really crossing guards, but I am not sure and need some levity here.

Unions represent and protect the bad teachers who are not accountable and who cannot be fired for substandard or inadequate performance. Because there are a lot of bad teachers in the public school system, you can't expect to have exceptional results from the students.

More importantly and an unintended consequence of a bad teacher being rewarded for a poor performance is that the truly outstanding teachers lose their desire to perform exceptionally or they just leave the teaching profession altogether. Unions protect and retain the weakest link in the food chain.

When the great and good teachers have to teach to lower standards implemented and promoted by union leadership, poor school administrators and bad teachers, you end up with an inferior school system which we have now. No government employees, federal, state, local should be allowed to participate in unions. No police, firefighters, EMS or other government employees paid for by tax dollars should be allowed to participate in unions. There are numerous reasons for this position which will become evident as you read further on.

If the unions are permitted for their original purpose to protect the employees, both public and private, against employer abuse and safety in the work place, that would be fine. Simply require that a union can't have collective bargaining or participate in negotiating compensation packages such as insurance or pensions and you will see the unions disappear. There will be no membership, no membership dues and no political votes that can be purchased.

This would be an excellent step towards improving the public school system. Compensation is an individual right for ones labor. It is only a collective right in a socialist/communist society. America is not a socialist/communist state. We are a democratic republic and no special interest should have unfettered access to the people's treasury!

The Best Electorate is an Ignorant Electorate
For the Socialist Progressive Democrat

The education system in America was going along fine until liberal curriculums, government interference and union self-interests started to make "progressive improvements" in the system. You can see the results of those improvements in America's educational decline; isn't this the perfect quintessential oxymoron

You would see education standards rise considerably if it was run as a business through the local communities without federal government intrusion or interference. The District of Columbia spends more money on primary and secondary education than any school district in the United State, yet they have one of the largest failure and dropout rates in the country. This is just one of many prime examples illustrating how throwing money at the problem is surely not the answer to anything, especially the decline in public education.

It is constantly reported through the media that public education is a dismal failure. For all the angst aired on behalf of our poor little children in this country by the politicians and the media, it seems that these simple problems would and could have been corrected a long time ago. We thought politicians, the mass media's unwavering support and excessive amounts of money were going to solve the crisis of inner city plantations too; but it has not. You can call it cynical, but maybe keeping people ignorant serves a different political purpose. Everything we've been discussing so far points in that direction.

Ignorance definitely helps keep those inner city plantations full and their inhabitants completely dependent on the government. What a web we weave. Doesn't it make you proud of your government, the public education system and your country?

This is not a conspiracy theory. It is just an acknowledgement of the power and greed that has infected our leaders in government. Socialist sympathizers in government and at fine colleges all over this country espouse the great societal visions and benefits of a socialist/communist state. They don't just study, preach and teach these visions but they advocate infamous historical figures that practiced them such as Hitler, Mao, Stalin, Che and Lenin.

The proponents of these potentially perfect societies espouse that it was not the fault of the socialist ideals which caused those societies to fail. It was the fault of the one carrying the banner. In other words, it wasn't that socialism is a failed social and economic system; it was just run incorrectly by Hitler, Mao, and Stalin when they implemented the system.

After the intentional murder of more than 100 million people by these socialist and communist regimes, you would think that someone would have gotten the benefits of socialism right. I guess no one is left to tell us how to get it right, because those who implemented these dictatorial governments killed off all those whom dissented. These systems failed even when there was no one left alive to dissent the actions of the socialist state oppression and control.

Our President and the far left base of the Socialist Democrat Party believe the vision of perfection is achievable if just given the chance to be executed properly....Again.
I am sure if they are able to completely and fundamentally transform this great nation, they will make the same mistakes, impose the same oppression and guarantee the complete collapse and failure of our country.

+It is regrettable because these socialist sympathizers have invested nothing of their own in this destructive folly and because of this America is on the verge of losing everything she has created. They have already increased the American debt on our citizens to 17 trillion dollars; a debt that will never be repaid prior to a complete economic collapse. Obama and his ilk have succeeded in stealing and redistributing our wealth to themselves.

Modern socialism is failing in Western Europe as you can see by the high unemployment, riots and chaos in the streets. The Germans are getting an idea of how America feels. All their neighbors are expecting them to bail them out from their underfunded entitlement programs and excessive civil servant union arbitrated employment and pension contracts. Foolishly the Germans are wasting their treasures like we in America are continuing to waste ours.

Poor Germany! They have elected and re-elected just enough socialist in their government like we have in America, who know what's best for them. They will steal from the German people's treasury and give it to the moochers in Germany and other countries in the European Union. Now these liberal regressives are trying to force these failed economic policies on us here in America. The socialist degenerates in our country are trying to kill capitalism in the only pure capitalistic society left on earth. It also happens to be the greatest and most powerful country on the planet. So why are the liberals so hell bent on destroying everything America stands for?

If they succeed, the moochers will have a new host of producers to chew on for a little while, and then America will no longer exist. The producers will have no reason to produce. Just like the good teachers, the producers will no longer stand around and take it. They will quit. This sad condition which is infecting our country is the product of the liberal elites in government, education and the media.

I don't mind that professors are allowed to teach their theories. I mind that they present these theories as fact to our children. I mind that there is not a balanced approach to teaching all sides of an issue. I find it repulsive that most university boards and chairs actively keep conservative professors of opposing views from being hired.

It is disgusting that our society has taken so many social and criminal degenerates and elevated them to hero status through professorships. Many hold posts at our most revered and prestigious liberal bastions like Berkley, Northwester, Columbia, Occidental and all the other Ivy's. They are given tenure thereby allowing them to teach subjects such as the justification for terrorism, civil disobedience, white privilege or eugenics with no accountability to anyone.

In closing this part on American education, it should be noted that these universities are given large tax breaks on their huge endowment funds which are supposed to be used to assist the less fortunate in receiving an education. These funds should be subject to annual government audits to make sure they are being used for their intended tax exempt purpose.

The funds are worth billions of dollars and used for many purposes beside scholarships. I think these funds should be used for their intended educational purposes only and should be strictly regulated. After all, they have been granted preferential tax exemptions to assist them in further advancing higher education in America. It seems evident that attaining success from their endeavors has completely eluded them.

We should also demand that the majority of these funds be used instead of hoarded in investment accounts. The interest that these funds accumulate through investment should be taxed at the maximum corporate rate. These behemoth tax shelters need to pay their fair share. Isn't this the socialist way? In addition, misuse or violations due to misuse of these funds should be grounds to lose their tax exempt status.

The responsibility for public education needs to be returned to the states and the local communities. The federal government should stop taxing the American people for education. The Department of Education should be abolished and all federal programs eliminated that pertain to education and educational support.

It is not a constitutional mandate for the federal government to be in the education business. It actually is a power left to the states that was commandeered by Congress. More importantly, the department and its programs are a complete waste of tax payer money with a meager if any positive return from the investment.

The federal experiment into public education has failed and generations of American children have suffered because of it. It is time to return to local public education, local public funding, local accountability and advanced academic curriculums for all American children.

Abolish the unions in education and develop a merit based pay system for teachers who excel in the classroom. Let the money follow the children instead of the schools. Poor performing schools would be forced to close their doors. Local government should set higher academic performance standards for all students, teachers and administrators in all school districts throughout America. These simple changes would represent real progress in the public education system in America.

Abortion

The Age of Reason

There is no one smarter than a teenager or a young open minded college student, young minds flying free through the queries of life, searching for the perfect life without a care in the world. In their quest for knowledge they look down on their parents and those who went before them... as a bunch of dumb rocks.

It is a natural biological instinct for the fledgling to jump out of the warm nest. If parents were perceived as smart or made it too comfy, these damn kids would never leave! Many of them are under the misimpression that we never want them to leave. If that is what they believe then you have miserably failed as a parent. No really, you failed as a parent!

Yes, I know, for I too have fond memories of my youth and the limitless power of my omnipresent brain. I was a liberal then. There were no absolutes, only shades of grey.
Then I grew up and saw the taxes coming out of my paycheck. BOOM!!!!! A conservative was born.

Once you escape the theories of college professors and participate in the world of reality, you come to some truly enlightening conclusions. Life's lessons are many. When you actually have a job where your ineptitude is not protected by union contracts, like school teachers, firefighters, policemen, local, state and federal employees, you brighten up pretty quick.

Your success or failure is your own and you own it. You find out what it means to sacrifice for others and give up luxuries to see your dreams grow. You learn from your mistakes or you are doomed to repeat them. You're thankful to those who helped you succeed and you don't look kindly on people who think they are entitled to what you sacrificed to achieve. You absolutely never see your government as being instrumental in your success. The only idiot that would believe that bullshit would have to hold political office; possibly even the presidency.

When you become a conservative you understand that government is a hindrance and never assisted you in attaining anything of value. You realize capitalism and a democratic republic is the best form of government ever conceived or implemented (Unless you are a diehard communist or socialist.) You also realize why America is the country every other country wants to be on one hand, but would love to see fail on the other. You grow up and become a conservative. Not a Republican mind you, but a true conservative.

During one of my enlightened periods, one of my brightest moments, it came to me that there aren't gray situations. There are only black and white situations. Black and white answers are like garlic is to vampires for liberal elites. You cannot manipulate black and white situations no matter how hard you try.

In order to profess liberalism, you have to have an open mind about everything. Then you have to agree that there is no right answer. I'm OK (liberal) you're OK (conservative), unless of course I'm not OK for the liberal, and then you are always wrong as the conservative. Hello out there! Now that you are listening we can talk about abortion.

The Losing Arguments for Abortion

I have heard all the reasons why abortion is not murder. Simply stated, you are wrong. It is murder. This is not a woman's body issue. This is however, a baby's body issue. This is not a euthanasia issue. This is not a discussion of the concept of when life begins. This is man's legalization of murder to assuage his/hers own guilt or ignorance for his/hers irresponsible actions.

It does not matter if it is the man's or the woman's fault for having unprotected sex and becoming pregnant. It only matters that the human being created as a result is going to be murdered to cover for the indiscretion and irresponsibility of another person or persons.

By claiming that the baby is not a baby, but is a mass of cells is jurist prudence for saying I was irresponsible and I need a fall guy to get me out of this problem through the legal system. Thus I will not be guilty of my religious sin or the legal act of murder. I am exonerated on all counts.

If you go back to the original intent of the law as presented to the American public regarding abortion you will find three justifications for aborting a pregnancy. The reasons given were to protect a woman from having a baby 1) conceived through incest, 2) conceived in the violent act of rape or 3) which would cause immeasurable harm or even death to mother from the pregnancy.

In these three cases and to the best of my knowledge, the only cases in all American history where a child could be killed legally in uteri were for the ultimate protection of the mother. It was never presented as a "right to her body" as proposed today. This "rights to her body issue" is a relatively new feminist contrived and endorsed concept.

The idea that it is a woman's right to murder her child and that abortion is acceptable as a preferred choice of contraception instead of a last resort is disgusting and enthusiastically condoned by the Democrat Party's ideology. It is a platform that appeals to the ignorant and irresponsible victims; the female base of the Democrat Party. This idea of absolved murder has been advanced mostly by unsavory far left elements lurking in the shadows of the Democrat party. The Democrats firmly believe in publicly funded abortion pandering to many of the poor and women in their base perfectly.

The abortion issue has been further marginalized by decisions rendered by judicial activist on the bench. We "progressed" from three simple methods of justified infanticide to a more complex system. We have added a number of situations which would justify and minimize the value of human life through our court system.

One of the first cases was to establish when life begins. In biology books and science text, life begins at the inception of the sperm penetrating the egg and creating a viable embryo. Enter scientific study, judicial review, case precedents, NOW and all the legal scholars of our time and the situation becomes quite blurred, gray and progressive if you will.

Some say it is a mass of cells that can be aborted at anytime. Others claim it is not a baby until it takes its first breath. You have professional politicians, legislators and judges who promote the belief that you can abort the baby from conception to full term. Others believe the baby can be aborted after this first trimester or second trimester. This maybe a prejudice statement, but some of your biggest proponents of abortion are women who are members of the Democrat Party. Are you surprised? I am not.

You even have the most intelligent man in the world who studied at Occidental and Harvard and became President of the United States propose legislation that would permit killing a live baby after the baby survived a botched abortion. A truly intellectual giant among men by all measure representing the progressive ideology of the extreme left in the Democrat Socialist Party.

So you can see that through political and judicial activism or liberal enlightenment and of course for the benefit of all society, to abort at any time it is *convenient* is acceptable. Coupled with the position of the victim and her right to her body, any murder or infanticide is completely appropriate and legal.

The baby is not a human being from conception, from birth, or until it is killed after being born alive to protect the doctor from a malpractice suit. However, even if found guilty, he won't be convicted of first degree murder; just the lesser charge of medical malpractice.

The gray matter from case law that further muddied the waters came down to a woman's right to her body. Whenever the subject is brought up it always goes back to the question: What do you expect a poor woman victim to do? I would expect her to give birth and give the baby up for adoption.

Here is a stellar idea. Maybe the father would actually want the baby! No, that is completely against the progressive policy. They need the state to be the baby's daddy. You could take the case as presented by the President in regards to abortion.

Paraphrasing the president, he said he would not want his daughters to suffer from an unfortunate mistake. We know what his legislative positions on abortion are, so his decision for his teenage daughters does not surprise me. What does surprise me is that in the 21st century after billions of tax dollars providing free access to public school sex education, free public school issued condoms, and the numerous choices, availability and unlimited access to his and hers methods of contraception, abortion is still on the increase, not the decrease.

The moral decay and sexual promiscuity that is beamed down from every social network and every form of media, to these "women" and "men", "girls" and "boys" reinforces the idea that they are <u>still</u> somehow victims of their mistakes. They are in reality, victims of their own ignorance and irresponsibility. In America today they are completely absolved from all responsibility for their actions or inactions.

Abortion is the center stone achievement to which all oppressed women victims have aspired; gender approved murder. Congrats to the Democrat party and all the liberal ladies on your progressive accomplishments. I am sure all of the 50 million or so dead babies would stand to salute you if they were actually here; but they are dead.

Abortion is murder plain and simple. It is not your right to kill another person because you housed it in your uterus. It may be a perceived privilege but it is by no means a right. The pregnancy in all likelihood was a consequence of intentional actions; two people having unprotected sex.

It is black and white. It is murder and no one should have the right to commit murder. The only victim, who really is a victim in our society, is the murdered child. More than 50 million have been killed since abortion was legalized. I don't think there were that many conceptions from incest, rape or potential health complications. I am also pretty sure it substantially exceeds the number of real victims that died in the concentration camps during the Nazi reign in Germany or the gassings in Iraq and Syria. Not such a great achievement when you look at it that way is it?

Eugenics in Practice

An important note in this discussion has to do with the study and practice of eugenics. It is a degenerative subversive platform of the socialist agenda. It has been practiced throughout time. The definition is as follows:

A science dealing with the "improvement" (as by selective breeding) of hereditary qualities especially of human beings.

Now you may look upon this definition and see the word improvement being a key word. It conjures up positive images like the words progressive, enlightened, refreshing etc. It also means negative things like white supremacy, Aryan race, pure race, genetic modification and methods used to eliminate an inferior race. In practice, it has been anything but positive.

Eugenics is morally reprehensible and incomprehensible in practice. Did you know there were government sponsored eugenics programs in the past in the United States? Did you know that the Hitler regime practiced experiments in eugenics seeking a superior German race? Did you know that in America, more black babies are aborted than white babies? Is the practice of abortion in America a racist program? It is definitely something to ponder.

Obamacare does have death panels. Whether they were provided for in the original 2,000 page atrocity or added as pork to one of the many stimulus packages, they are in the law. Sarah Palin didn't lie and isn't quite as ignorant and stupid as Katie Couric appears to be. These panels are responsible for rules and guidelines. They are appointed again, by the Executive, and are the scapegoats for politicians, if they make a medical decision that upsets the electorate.

The politicians will not be held accountable for the decisions of these panels. The members will be dressed down and put on public display then they will get immunity from the politicians they protect. They will be returned to their jobs rationing health care and deciding who is important enough to live or die. They will comprehensively decide who dies; the old, the infirm, the mentally ill, the babies that survived abortion, or children without blue eyes.

Will these people be of no value because they can no longer produce taxes to throw in the bottomless pit of the US Treasury? What political hack will determine ones viability? Someone as inept as the current Secretary of Health and Human Services, Kathleen Sebelius? In fact, it may be determined that these people are worthless because they drain the resources out of the Treasury.

Just a quick note on good ol' Kathleen SS. Kathleen Sebelius's claim to fame was as the Democrat Governor of Kansas where the notorious Dr. Tiller performed late term abortions with Kathy's blessing. She received large campaign donations from Dr. Tiller and is a strong outspoken advocate of the pro choice band. Is this life time political hack the one you want overseeing the government death panels being implemented through Obamacare? She sure the hell isn't someone I'd want administering my health care!!

These same types of "man made corruptible panels" killed Jesus Christ, the Christians in the coliseum, the Jews in Germany, the Muslims during the Crusades and the witches of Salem. Do you have blue eyes?

Since death panels are in fact an intricate part of Obamacare, an appointed panel could decide that one race may be superior to another race and make the other races expendable? Why does the use of these eugenic programs seem so unreasonable? I mean, let's be clear, they are for the improvement and forward progress of the human race. They have been used by our government and other governments before. Why would you be surprised that they would not be used again?

The most diabolical animal on the planet is man. The most easily led animal to slaughter on the planet is an uneducated poor man subject to an evil and corrupted government. You can bet that the government is going to say these forays in eugenics were all for the good of the country. That is what Hitler told them as he sent many a poor soul into the showers.

Eugenics is a practice that makes sure only people that can produce the most for the state are worth being born. The same decision makers or politicians that will allow for you to live will be the same decision makers or politicians that will decide when you will die. By systematically eliminating inferior people the government will be able to keep coffers full and skyrocketing costs under control. That is currently how our government gets what they want when they want it. It's for your own good stupid!

When they succeed in reaching their ultimate goal of a government administered single payer insurance system, or by implementing some other form of bastardized Obamacare, the federal government will simply withhold or deny your medical care. Eugenics and managed health care are both programs that have historical significance and provide a terrifying window into our probable future.

Legalized Murder Should Be Abolished

What do I think? A woman should have the baby and give it up for adoption. A young girl and the baby's father should be home schooled until she gives birth or be sent to an alternative school. The "mistake" should not be accommodated, highlighted and accepted as normal practice and forced on one's classmates.

The girl and her baby daddy should not be assimilated back into school while they are pregnant. I know this is a huge inconvenience on the girl, the boy and more than likely the parents, or a single parent, but that is the result of their actions. Hopefully, at the very least it will stop another unwanted pregnancy and be an example for others.

If you are an adult when you get pregnant, both the man and his sex partner should pay for the mother's medical care and any other related expenses until the baby is born and then put the baby up for adoption. In these scenarios, I am assuming that the woman and the man did not want the baby, but don't condone murder either. Maybe abortion won't be an option in the future except for the original reasons it was _legally_ proposed and enacted.

I realize that abortions have been practiced throughout time and that making them illegal will not stop the hideous practice. In addition, I still believe there are valid reasons for aborting a child due to incest, rape or preserving a woman's health or life. These are legal justifications, not religious justifications. Those judgments are better left up to a higher Deity.

In these dire cases, the woman is truly a victim of unfortunate circumstance and her life should be saved over the life of her baby. Then if we are judged wrong, we will be judged by the Creator instead of some creature as imperfect as man. But to allow abortions as contraception of convenience is unacceptable, completely immoral and totally wrong. It is murder. I think Congress should revisit the law and rewrite it; protecting the woman and protecting the innocent child. Murder by abortion should be the exception to the rule and it should not be flippantly promoted, accepted and practiced.

The Reconstruction of the Extended American Family

American Men and Fathers

The demise of the American extended family accelerated in the 1960's. Deviant behavior rose out of the ashes of Woodstock and the most degenerate members of the deviant class replaced what was normal in our society. For every one positive step forward, the pendulum swung two steps back. This has been the liberal view of progress.

Today's elite academics were coming of age during the 60's period, and now they are passing on their progressive political poison to our young. So you know where this is going and it "ain't" pretty.

I know I have said this before but I have to hammer this point home. The importance of the family unit was destroyed for the purpose of individual self-fulfillment. I am not saying that self-fulfillment is not important to one's happiness and success in life. It is necessary to love one's self in order to love and care for others. You cannot love another until you love yourself first. Even Jesus said, "Love thy neighbor as thyself." He assumed you loved yourself and that you would love others accordingly.

However, self-fulfillment at the expense of others is narcissistic and hedonistic. It is self-fulfillment run amok. It is the "two steps" back. This may sound extreme, but the destruction of the extended family is an unintended consequence of the "free love "era, Civil rights era and the Women's Liberation movement. It is important to analyze the positive and negative effects of the 60's on the "progressive development" of each individual member which comprised the extended family.

Progressive in this book is not the same as the definition you would find in the dictionary. The definition you would find in the dictionary would be a positive concept. No. " Progressive" in this book is strictly in reference to an innocuous canker on the ass of every American citizen.

It is a political perversion finding domicile in the Democrat party. They are biblically equivalent to a party that would produce, promote and support the Anti-Christ. As a political party, many of the umber far left in the party would be the equivalent of the KKK, the Russian KGB or Hitler's Third Reich. In reality, they would never represent a religious group, even radical Islam, because they are proponents of secularism. You can be assured they are destroying America under the banner of fundamental transformation.

These deviants have infiltrated the Executive, Legislative and Judicial branches of our federal government and are openly working to fundamentally change our country into something unrecognizable.

Before getting started in this discussion it should be noted that prior to the 1960's the family structure was known to be an extended family. The unit was multi-generational including grandparents, uncles, aunts, cousins, brothers and sisters living in close proximity to one another.

The elderly were taken care of by the other family members when they were too ill to care for themselves. Many family problems and issues such as drug abuse where handled within and by this type of family unit. They did not look, nor did they expect, nor would they accept government intervention or interference in their lives. They didn't air their dirty laundry in public. They kept certain problems in the closet and contained within the family. Personal privacy was an American right and it was treasured as such.

That all changed when the 1960's put the final nail in the coffin of the extended family. The self-fulfillment decade left little time for others problems. The "all about me" generation abandoned the old, and ever so progressively, their young to government's care. In case you haven't picked this up yet, the government as it exists in America today is a socialist pariah sucking all the treasures out of America and replacing the void with ignorant deviant indigents.

Thus we have created the new and improved progressive version of the American family- The nuclear family. Originally that was dad, mom, and 2.1 children. But now it has progressed again. It is now, YOU. Yes, it is all about you all the time.

You have now progressed into the statist version of an individual and been placed in a class of like individuals. Now that we have you delineated into your class we can mold you into progressive compliance.

We are classed by types of victimhood. We are specifically delineated into races, gender or religion and we are all victims in this new "YOU" society. Our children are victims of divorce and wards of the state. Men are the perpetrators of the crime of victimhood and therefore cannot be classed as victims. There is only one gender and race which cannot be a victim in America and that is the white male. There is only one victim that trumps a black American male in our society and that is a woman of any race or creed.

The father in American culture was the patriarch and head of the household. There were a multitude of cultures that came ashore in this great country, and how fathers played their roles varied greatly. However, the man was the head of the household.

He was a masculine male, bread winner, husband, friend, father, protector and in many cases the last word. Like all situations of dominance whether assigned, expected, real or perceived, the father could be a positive or a negative influence in the family the same as any other family member. Some say that the role of father prior to the 1960's precluded participation in child rearing. I disagree and feel that is a sexist interpretation, again rising out of the dung heap of the 60's and the women's liberation movement.

Professors have been spending decades trying to prove these discriminations. However, nothing could be further from the truth. Liberals and women may not have appreciated the traditional roles of fatherhood, but to say they had no place or a negative place in the raising of the children is not true. The father was and still is an integral part of a properly functioning family.

In fact, there isn't a family unit without a father, only a dysfunctional shell. The father has his own set of responsibilities, uniquely male I might add, to perform in order for the family unit to thrive and succeed. You need look no further than the inner city streets to see the multitudes of juvenile delinquents who are suffering from not having a father in their lives. Father figures, mentors and step dad's are also inadequate substitutions from having one's own father in the home. A father is extremely important to a child's development and security.

Many fathers prior to the 1960's would take their children to school on the way to work, participate in extracurricular activities after school, and assist them with their homework, just like fathers today. They would deal with discipline and other assorted domestic situations when they arose. The father would act as an authority figure and disciplinarian in the home with regards to the children misbehavior. A good husband would support his wife and as a team they would raise their children, thus sharing the childrearing responsibilities. Ozzie and Harriet were fiction then and they are fiction now.

The roles of the father and mother were different but complementary. Chances are a troubled teenage son or daughter would be more disrespectful and belligerent to his or her mother than to his or her father. Not much has changed there, so we can assume this adolescent behavior is biologically wired in the brain.

A good father would come to the mother's defense. Thus the old adage "wait until your father gets home" was born. I don't think that expression was pertinent to a rebellious 3 year old and a father's intervention in that case was probably not a necessity. Mom handled that one on her own.

Yes, the cohesiveness of the extended family was dependent on a strong father and strong mother in the home. They were a team. Today there are few teams left. Remember there is no "I" in team for "I" stands for individual and individual stands for ME; It's all about ME!

A father figure in the home has been proven to provide stability and support to the entire family unit. Children need a father and their development is better with a loving and caring father around. A fatherless home or a motherless home is not a complete home. It may be functional, acceptable and even promoted as normal (which it is not), but it is not ideal for raising a child. It's a damn hard and important job to raise a child and it takes at least two normal adult parents to have any chance for success. Normal is the operative word here so it leaves us plenty of leeway. If there isn't any yeast in the bread, the bread isn't going to rise. It is not a complete family without a father.

Supplementing the roles of either parent, with same sex relationships, does provide added stability for some children; however it is not equivalent to a husband and wife marriage. I am a proponent of civil unions on a secular level. However, I believe marriage is a religious institution. In the end, for many of us, we believe God will be the final judge.

But trying to equate a same sex family unit with a man/ woman family unit is like trying to force a square peg through a round hole. The government is an expert at trying this type of social engineering. Even if you have the tools to make the hole bigger, it doesn't make it right; it falls outside the normal bounds of nature.

Progressives site all kinds of studies and polls to support their positions. Usually those studies are paid for by Progressives and provided by those in Progressive towers of higher learning. Polls can be biased and found to support almost any number of positions. Therefore I do not give a lot of credit to polls when analyzing different positions. Liberals believe providing a loving and nurturing environment to a child by two loving people is all that is necessary to successfully raise a child. No, I disagree; it takes a lot more than two people to succeed in raising a child. It takes a family; not a village, commune or work farm.

I do agree some same sex couples and even some single parent households can raise children effectively but that it is not the ideal situation. It is a black and white situation made gray to accommodate a societal position of acceptance regarding same sex unions and the prevalence of divorce.

I would still rather see a child reared by two loving and caring people instead of one. It is an extremely difficult job to raise children with many important responsibilities which have to be consistently performed. Raising a child to adult hood takes time, energy, intelligence, patience and an understanding of the uniqueness of each child we blessed to be given. However, I don't agree that because same sex or single parenting has been deemed acceptable by a minority in our society, that these situations are equal to or better than a healthy marriage between a father and mother, male and female.

It is acceptable in our society to have same sex unions, but that is a socially and legally based determination. It is socially acceptable and contractually legal for same sex couples to adopt. These are not biological determinations.

Biologically and by design in the animal kingdom, a male and a female of our species procreate and raise their young. This unit has evolved through time and been deemed a family. This is not homophobic. It is a fact. It is ok if you do not support my position. I don't support yours either. But we should be able to amicably disagree on some of these moral and social issues. This is what we are free to do in America. My point here is the importance of the father in the family and the way his traditional role has been demonized by the liberal progressives. The father figure had to be minimized to achieve the final goal; breakdown of the American family and the destruction of the middle class.

The importance of the father figure is indisputable, even if conditions don't always warrant a father in the home. My problem with one outcome of the 1960's is that divorce has become acceptable and even preferred resolution to marriage problems in American society. The ease with which one can break this moral commitment and legal contract has been very detrimental to our society. It reinforces the concept of not having to take responsibility for ones actions.

It minimizes the importance of a contract between two people. If you don't fulfill your legal obligations, and the other party has no recourse for attaining justice, then there is no reason to enter a contract. If there is no commitment or legal recourse from a legal contract, marriage or civil unions, are not necessary; no one is responsible, no rule, no foul.

These legal contracts and personal commitments are the foundation for the creation of the family unit. The religious issue is a separate argument; albeit an important one. If this disregard for law proceeds, then state recognized marriages and civil unions will be eliminated completely. There will be no laws to govern cohabitation, copulation or the complete dissolution of the family unit. Wait, we are already there!

This I believe is another goal of the progressive ideology. By making it easy to dissolve the family structure it allows a vacuum to be created which will be filled by the government as the sole provider.

It has been said that divorce is better for the family because the remaining family would be better off without parental tension and marital discourse in the home. That opinion doesn't address the unintended consequences of remarriage, delinquency, or the social stigmatism associate with coming from a divorced family.

The Liberal Democrats solution to this inconvenient stigmatism is to make sure most children come from broken homes through the acceptance of divorce as normal. The birth of the, "no fault" divorce and the grounds of "irreconcilable differences" were instrumental in helping achieve this result. It made it even easier to destroy the family unit and in the void, a fully dysfunctional and morally deficient home was left in place as planned.

Divorces should be difficult. They should require couples to be responsible to their familial and contractual obligations. The reason there is a stigmatism on divorce because it isn't ok. It is a personal failure.

The courts rule on the contractual obligations for financial compensation in divorce cases. I think visitation and visitation schedules are an over reach of their legal authority and a form of judicial activism.

If there is no case of abuse, the child should be able to see the non-custodial parent at any time. Sorry if it's not acceptable to the one who has been given custody, but they may have to get over their bitterness and deal with the inconvenience of schedule changes for the benefit of the child. The child should not be punished because the parents broke their contracts and commitments to each other. What kind of lessons do we teach our children when we don't feel the need or desire to fulfill our obligations?

Additionally, another degenerate progressive outcome of the liberation era was that certain indiscretions, such as adultery, were looked upon as incidental not morally repugnant. It was the "if you can do it, I can do it too!" It seemed to be that two wrongs did make it right. Women cheat on men as easily as men cheat on women in today's society. It's not considered morally reprehensible if both sexes can do it. Right!?

The father deserted his responsibilities or the mother deserted hers. All made possible through the teachings of free love and the communal acceptance that was so prevalent during the sex decade. The marriage commitment, the moral obligation, and the legal contract between two consenting adults, all were disregarded with little or no negative consequences to the parties of the contract. Kind of like the government bailouts of GM and Chrysler...or the banks....or Freddie Mae and Freddie Mac....or....no consequences for one's actions just bailouts; just more pathetic victims.

Of course, there were financial remedies worked out in the courts. It must be alright because the government made you pay for it. But there were and are far worse outcomes that result from divorce. There are innocent third parties involved that have to emotionally pay for those divorces often for the rest of their lives.

The children of divorced parents have the very foundations of their existence ripped out from under them. Children need a strong foundation. They need limits. They process change in more intense fashion than adults because that is how a child's mind normally works. Divorce is traumatic for any child.

The father and mother are the pillars on which the child's foundation is built. The fight and incentive to stay together, in good times and bad, should be preferable and more intensely fought for than to settle for the easy way out; divorce. This is true for both parties in the marriage.

The destruction of the extended family by downsizing to the nuclear family was bad enough for America. But removing the father and/or mother, replacing them with a government bureaucrat parent, completely dismantles the family unit and destroys the positive foundations for individual development. This again is the progressive socialist plan.

There were adverse social changes for white men that resulted from the 1960's. The white male was the culprit held responsible for the need to implement the Civil Rights movement. He was and still is emasculated by women, the media, the liberal sociology and psychology professors, and of course, the whore class of elected officials made up of diverse and divisive classes of America's victims. This persecution of the white man is still prevalent and encouraged among the ranks of victims in our society.

The white male is to blame for all that is wrong in American and he will find no maternal compassion sent his way. No one else is responsible. All the problems are his fault; Boo Friggin Hoo! The majority of what remains is a bunch of beaten down, effeminate, androgynous, metro-sexual wimps where proud men once stood.

These injustices and inequalities imposed on women were second only to the victims of the Civil rights movement. In order to achieve equality between the sexes, we had to even the playing field quickly by imposing quotas, sex discrimination rules and laws, affirmative action and reverse discrimination programs. A whole array of new progressive government programs were forced on the American family.

Men couldn't appear to discriminate against women or race. Men couldn't tell jokes with sexual content at work, tell someone they looked nice or you were labeled a sexist chauvinist pig and potentially liable to defend yourself in court.

This was not the case for a woman and still isn't. You hit the victimhood trifecta if you are a woman, a woman of color, and a homosexual. Pedophile male school teachers are vilified and pedophile female school teachers are glorified. Ok. That is an exaggeration, but not much of one.

As always government made sure to interfere and make all things right in the world. Since NOWv (National Organization of Women Victimhood) is still active, I can assure you that somewhere out there, a liberated female victim needs to be rescued (Sandra Fluke)...unless you're straight conservative women who believes in God, marriage or takes stand against abortion.

Don't take this the wrong way, but there were and still are many women out there who are over sensitive on these issues. Damn, that was sexist, you white male prick! Could that be a legitimate difference between the sexes...maybe?! Men do not get offended as easily as many women do. It must be that victimhood, glass ceiling, and the even playing field thing we men have heard so much about since Women's Suffrage and the 1960's bra burnings.

"How does that make you "FEEL" Hon? Women calling me derogatory names don't offend me and I don't "feel" like a victim from their verbal assaults. These liberated women are much more reasonable when their hormones are in balance. Damn, I did it again! I can't help myself...time for some diversity training. You can always spot a liberated woman because she can't take any type of sexist joke and is the first and loudest to whine about it.

In order to save all the oppressed (NOWv, Cosmo, Vogue, Move On Org) from the white male, the great liberal minds of America turned to the victim/socialist playbook written for the Civil Rights Movement. They just changed the words from "black" to "women." There was and there still is no tolerance for any white man to say that any woman was different from a man. It was even unacceptable (and still is) to state that the sexes were biologically, physiologically or psychologically different from one another. It doesn't matter even if is factually true. (Which it is) If you profess it long enough, the uneducated entitled sheep will believe it.

If you are an American male, you can't question a women's right to her body to the extent that the US Supreme Court ruled that she could legally murder a person through abortion. If the Supreme Court, with their uniquely qualified female jurists declare abortion legal, then they must be right. It is right up there with the absurd split decision to allow Obamacare to stand as a form of taxation. It is even harder to believe that someone didn't get to Chief Justice Roberts before he cast the final vote. Something just doesn't' smell right there.

Even though discriminatory conditions may have existed that needed to be rectified, the way in which attempts were made to correct the problems went beyond politically correct. Based on the progressive pendulum theory, we are now successfully taking four steps backwards.

Liberal progressivism went to the absurd. You would think the suffrage movement culminating with a constitutional amendment allowing women to vote would have put women on the same footing with men. No, that right wasn't enough to equalize the playing field; once a victim always a victim.

Instead, the white male became the women liberation scapegoat and another group of victims were added to the ever growing pool of victimhood. Another class of division accomplished and promoted by the Democrat party and socialist progressive movement.

Finally, Caucasian men have had their roles and place in American society redefined by all the victims. They seemed to have lost their identity and morphed into pseudo black men or much worse, androgynous urban confused "metro sexuals." I thought a metro sexual was a pervert that got turned on by subway turnstiles. No they are result of being pussy whipped by liberal progressives and the victims they represent.

These faux males are a form of male which promote Democrat progressive movement ideology. In seeking their new and acceptable identity many white males have turned to the black male thug as a role model. The problem with white males emulating black males is that white males are picking up the entire group of negative attributes, and none of the positive attributes which black men have to offer in American Society.

Black men are excellent scholars, entertainers, athletes and also exceptional fathers, friends and mentors. There are many great Americans like Col. West, Tyler Perry, Dr. Ben Carson and Martin Luther King Jr. I will acquiesce that even though I don't agree with their liberal socialist policies, their attempts to race bait and destroy America, President Obama, Colin Powell, Bill Clinton and even Juan Williams must have some redeeming qualities to have reached their prospective pinnacles of success. I have just failed to recognize any of them.

Why do we white males emulate the lowest dregs in the black culture? Rap criminals, gang bangers, pants hanging below our fat asses, piercings and tattoos? Why don't we hold up and emulate the black men who have been successful role models like Bill Cosby, Clarence Thomas and Herman Cain in our society?

It is a problem created by a secular liberal "progressive" society when we hold up and idolize the deviants and degenerates of any class, race or culture. It is an ignorant society that wants us to accept mediocre as the norm. It shouldn't be this way. We need a strong and caring father figure and role model for our kids.

In addition, white men and black men, all American men in general, are losing all there masculine uniqueness and strengths to an asexual one-gender based society. There seems to be an attempt to socially meld the genders into sameness through social indoctrination by government, the media, special interest groups and public education.

It's not physically possible no matter how hard government, the media and the perceived victims try to make it happen. Men should teach their sons to be men and their daughters to be women. There is no shame in having "a set", taking your place and performing your responsibilities as husband, father, partner, mentor and an upstanding American in our society.

Too many young white men are increasingly joining the roles of the entitled moocher class. They are coming from fatherless homes. They are unemployed, under employed, under educated, dropping out and becoming wards of the state. Another socialist success story is being written for which we can all thank the Democrat Party.

Physically, young white males are being tattooed, body pierced all over, wearing their pants below their asses, holding their crotches and swaggering like pimps from the inner city plantations. If that is a positive aspect of black culture I fail to see it. If that is what America is becoming we have already lost the war.

You can call it cultural, but it isn't American and it isn't African. It is a result of cultural and social decay and it is not limited to the black community. It is infecting our entire society. This isn't a racial issue. It is a deviant and degenerate strain of American culture that is destroying this country and its youth. *Yes, it is the parents fault.* But the government has been offering their unsolicited assistance since they first broke into the Treasury to provide government subsidies and welfare.

I would be surprised if white male crime statistics aren't on the rise. It is pathetic that the majority in America is lowering our standards to the most deviant elements in our society. This is true for all of America. It is not color or gender specific but is deliberately being instituted through liberal progressive political design.

America, we have lost our way and need to find if we are going to be the once great nation we were before. We need to reconstitute the virtues and foundational integrity of America by rebuilding the extended family into our society. We need to love and care for all members of our family and protect them from becoming wards of the state. It is our responsibility to take care of own in America.

The father figures need to be reinstalled at the head of the family. The foundation and protector of those he loves and cares for the most. He needs to be responsible for his actions and inactions. He needs to be the father he was meant to be and he needs to replace the government father that has replaced him; the same government that destroyed the extended and nuclear family.

American men don't need to take the bullshit heaped upon them by the fake victims created by a failed progressive movement. You don't have to fall prey to the liberal socialist agenda that has infected our great American society. You don't need to subject yourself or accept the propaganda put forth by a media staffed with affirmative action victims and far left liberal faux journalist indoctrinated in the utopian vision of socialism fresh out of journalism school. You don't need to submit to or accept the actions of any corrupt form of government.

Men in America need to stand up and take your place at the head of your family. You need to be a partner, friend, husband to you wife. You need to be a loving father and mentor to your children. But more importantly, you have to take a stand and kick the government out of your home, take your freedom, liberty and place back as a father in the foundation of America! That is what the American father was and should be again. Some things are not what they appear to be and are really not progressive at all. Take your place!

American Women and Mothers

When I was writing this chapter I knew I would catch all kinds of hell. No I am not a woman hater. Women in general take criticism a little more personally than most men do. I love women. I just don't believe in victimhood or that a woman is any more special or superior than a man.

Women in America wear the cloak of victimhood like an expensive new pair of Prada's. Victimhood dies hard and nobody wants to travel back to a time of suppression or oppression; real or perceived. Victimhood always blocks true progress.

But if we are going to move forward and understand the equality that is being sought, it is necessary to pull in the proverbial claws and review our history. If you can't do this calmly and rationally, then you probably shouldn't be reading this book. If you can't read this calmly and rationally, you probably voted for Obama and Clinton and are already fully enveloped in socialist thought. Stop reading now, you are closed minded and completely brainwashed. I sincerely appreciate that you were able to make it this far. Good bye, See ya later; for the rest read on.

Look at the way women who don't agree with Ann Coulter treat her. She is extremely intelligent, very attractive, ferociously independent and highly successful. She seems to be everything that the female victim has aspired to become. Yet she is belittled and attacked as some kind of ignorant conspiracy theory fanatic. The same way the media tries to depict the Tea Party and conservatives in general.

If a man treated Ann Coulter the way that many liberal women do, then the hags at NOWv and the likes of Andrea Mitchell and Rachel "Johnny Bravo" Maddow would be all over him and not in a good way either; no they would not. They would choose to ignore the story or be totally sympathetic to the man and say he was correct to disrespect and attack a trollop (using any number of catty expletives) like that conservative Ann Coulter.

The way the she wolfs in the press and the entertainment industry mercilessly attacked Sarah Palin is a prime example of media bias against conservative women. The press would never and have never said anything remotely disparaging about Michelle Obama or Hillary Clinton.

Do you think these liberal women find it hard to look at themselves in the mirror? I seriously doubt any liberal progressive political or press whore would have a problem self pimping in public or in a mirror; male or female. In any case, this part of the analysis is about the importance of most women and their many virtuous roles in the multi-faceted fabric that makes up America.

People still wallow in the memories of injustice which were the catalyst for the Civil Rights movement. Slavery was outlawed 100 years ago, the real victims died long after that time. But it doesn't take much to stir the ambers of anger on that subject. Jesse and Al are rattling sabers as you're reading this book.

The real tragedy was during the slavery period and Reconstruction. What we are experiencing today is a tried and true liberal tactic of victimhood and subjugation at the hands of government. The victim card is much more useful when you want to get your way in America.

We Americans are a compassionate people and are always on the side of the victim. We seek retribution from the offender, even if tried in a criminal court of law and found innocent, the American public are quick to seek justice.

An over emotional journalist or anchor (gender not specific) from the liberal media is always at the ready, waiting around the corner to help sensationalize the next victim. Everybody is a victim-except white men, Conservatives (men or women) or Christians (men or women).

The victim is always right even before all the facts are gathered (OJ/Trayvon). They never create their own problems; nor are they ever responsible for their actions. The liberal racists always demand swift justice for their victim's alleged grievances at everyone else's expense. The only one faster than trial attorney to exploit a poor victim is a concerned and compassionate politician with a panting and slobbering press in tow.

Women, throughout time, have always been in the victim class. They definitely have a number of legitimate complaints on that subject. They have been subjugated, enslaved and oppressed since before the time of Moses. It all goes back to that damn apple in the Garden of Eden.

No seriously, women were and still are possessions in South America, Africa, Asia and the Middle East. These societies are based on rule by patriarchs. These men rule in political and religious parties that form tribes, theocracies, monarchies and other forms of government including socialism and communism providing legal and religious doctrine in which to keep women enslaved, oppressed and under their complete control. European cultures were patriarch based and so were early American cultures.

However, America has real freedom and liberties provided for all Americans in her founding documents and American women have the ability to continue in their quest for equality. They have sought, fought and won their freedom, liberty and opportunity because they wanted to participate in the making of our great nation.

They wanted to enjoy freedom, life and the pursuit of happiness. They did not want to be second class citizens or continue on as someone's possession. They did not want to be under a man but next to him and the 19th Amendment was their vehicle and victory. Their victory was a victory for all of America.

We have always been a compassionate and caring people in America. We eventually get our problems resolved, much too often reverting to extreme regressive measures to achieve these goals; more times than not with some regressive unintended consequences.

We already discussed the bias created by quotas and affirmative action. They are not progressive and cause far more damage than cures in our society. The US Constitution however provided the 19th Amendment giving women the right to vote and empowering them to change America through their vote. It made them equal, at least legislatively and in the eyes of the law

There is one problem in America that persists in regards to women. American women couldn't or will not give up their ace in the hole- victimhood. Victimhood takes any perceived grievance and makes it an automatic egregious and unjust act as well.

As you know, female politicians must act expeditiously throwing the victim card whenever there is any kind of act committed against the poor female victim. As sexist as this may sound, women today abuse the use of victim scenario.

Women are the first to come to the aid of other victims when it comes to children, police, firefighters and the holy grail of all victimhood; the little old gray haired school teacher. This is not meant to be a blanket statement for all women. The term "women" is being used generically so don't "feel" like you are being personally attacked; unless the shoe fits of course.

Women in America use the victim card like some people use accusations of racism. When you can't prove your point intellectually or conclusively, you hide behind the race or victim card typical of the Democrat Party playbook page 1 Item 1. This is normally done to illicit some outrageous and rousing response from the crowd to divert from one's own ignorance.

It also makes for good TV and media coverage while diverting people's attentions from the person losing in an intelligent debate. The presentation of the victim is often over emotional, melodramatic and sensationalized which adds to the entertainment value of media coverage. It is attune to watching episodes of Nancy Grace or the daytime soap, Divorce Court. It is not that you murdered your two year old child; it is that you are a woman who couldn't handle the pressures of motherhood. You are the real victim not the baby you killed. The victim is never responsible.

Let's look at some of the achievements that have actually benefited women. The first and only valid one to truly advance all women in America was the Suffrage Movement and the implementation of the 19th Amendment. The following are not successes but are actually actions that have not benefited the women's movement in America, or if they did it was at a cost of someone else.

The creation of NOWv (National Organization of Women victimhood) is a leftist radical liberal group of confused women with gender identification issues. They supposedly represent all women groups and stand up for all women's grievances. However, they do not represent anything remotely female who believes in conservative values, pro life, Christianity or strict moral standards.

They whine and bellow in unison anytime a woman who is conservative, pro-life, or happily married, starts to gain ground on issues that NOWv doesn't endorse. I seriously believe many women in this organization want to be men and are quite successful at it. This organization of frustrated and frigid women represents the classic case of penis envy. They do not just want to achieve equal status. They think they can surpass equality.

They endorse leftist losers like Diane Feinstein, Babs Boxer, Nancy Pelosi, Billary, Lil Debbie Wasserman-Shultz and other progressive derelicts and liberal clingers like Sandra Fluke. These same female hypocrites turn on their own gender, condemn, ridicule and spread vicious lies about and against conservative icons such as Meg Whitman, Condoleezza Rice, Ann Coulter, Michelle Malkin and Sarah Palin. These progressive liberals would like to have a penis on them instead of in them and they would still expect someone else to pay for their contraception.

Women have suffered greatly because of the Sex Free 60's too. The biggest achievements they gained were the liberation of the tatas, the breakdown of the American family unit and legally justified gender approved murder.

This was the great era when woman gained the right to murder unborn babies with the blessing of the US Supreme Court in the case of Roe vs. Wade. This has been the greatest accomplishment for the progressives and women in our society. Women everywhere should be extremely proud of their legislative achievement; a legal absolution for women to commit infanticide.

Abortion is one of those unintended negative consequences in a woman's quest for freedom to control her own body. This true and complete freedom was only achieved at the cost of killing her baby. So be it! Right? After all it's her body and she doesn't have to be held responsible for her actions. She is after all the victim.

This victimhood position would be easy grounds for allowing abortions if there weren't a number of alternative forms of contraception available to women. Since there are alternatives doesn't that prove my point that abortion is nothing more than legal form of pre-meditated murder? Doesn't a woman have an alternative choice of contraception available? It is just a thought to ponder while sitting in the Planned Parenthood waiting room.

There have been several regressive strides backwards too such as Title IX. It was intended to be a positive move forward for women, but it had some negative unforeseen and unintended consequences too. It was an admirable endeavor into equality. It was meant to ensure equality or provide a step up for women, and it did, but at a cost to others. The others that it costs were namely men, the non victim class, so it is completely acceptable that men are still footing those costs. This is where things go wrong when the government intercedes.

Here's an example of what I am mean. Funds (TV endorsements, gate fees, alumni participation etc.) earned through a successful football or baseball program at Sucker University by the men's programs were "redistributed" (Obama vocabulary for theft) to sports programs for women. This was mandated by Title IX. It's was the only fair thing to do in the name of equality.

If you didn't subsidize (think government here) the women's program, you couldn't have a men's program. This is how the government would punish those who didn't comply. The public funds as well as the gate fees, TV fees and other endorsements earned by the men's programs would have to be diverted to the women's programs. The funds confiscated from the men's programs were "redistributed" to the women's programs. OK, we get it.

The equal playing field would allow women sports funding to catch up to men's sports funding with the hope that someday the women's programs would be self-sufficient and self-funded. This is the same concept behind issuing the Solyndra grants.

The majority of women's programs have not become self-sustainable since Title IX was passed. Monies are still being "redistributed" at a cost to the men's programs; in the name of equality and progress of course.

So in essence, it is and was ok to discriminate against a male if he doesn't get an athletic scholarship as long as a woman gets an athletic scholarship all for the greater good of society. Is this equality? No, it is a form of social promotion and sex discrimination. It is a form of socially engineered welfare. It is the same progressive ideology used to promote sameness when equality can't be achieved.

Even though the women's programs couldn't raise enough funds to support themselves, they were and remain subsidized by mandatory government requirements imposed on the American education system. The federal government will threaten to withhold education funding if the public educational institutions do not stay in compliance.

This is how victims of inequality are taken care of by government in America. Women are perceived as being in the victim class. If a women's program cannot generate enough funds, interest or success to be self-sufficient by the women in these programs, the government will prop it up through subsidies (welfare/entitlements). It is that "according to one's needs thing" Democrats are so proud of. It is a path to social justice through socialist dogma. These inequities are some of the unintended and negative consequences of Title IX. In many cases these negatives supersede the positives of the initial programs they were intended to correct.

The federal government funds abortion with tax dollars to Planned Parenthood even though Planned Parenthood vehemently denies the use of those funds for abortions. Planned Parenthood would cease to exist without government subsidies under the guise of helping the poor and indigent women in the inner city plantations. These socialist based policies and statist subsidized programs are actually regressive and hurt women more than they help as do most welfare and entitlement programs. They provide a hand out not a hand up.

Another case of women victimization was in the work place. Women were treated unjustly in the work place. In fairness and historical accuracy, women and children were subject to horrible work conditions in early American life. They worked tirelessly in sweatshops and factories for low wages and no benefits. They were not paid equally with their fellow male laborers doing the same jobs. If women didn't work and operate our factories during the wars America may have lost some if not all of them.

Roles for women began to change considerably during and after WWII. The traditional roles in the extended family and the domestic roles in the home were changing. Many urban households were moving and becoming suburban households. A larger portion of the female population began working outside the home. America was indeed changing for the better.

Women were seeking advanced degrees and enjoying greater access to educational opportunities. Their undeniable value during the war effort showed that women were quite capable of more than domestic chores. American men were begrudgingly ready to accept these changing roles; some sooner than others. It is natural for people to resist change. It is also true that all change is not necessarily good; but good or bad, major changes were occurring for women and men in America for sure.

Glass ceilings were implemented to keep women in their place at work. These ceilings were a form of discrimination instituted by men in the work force. In some offices there were naked pictures of women or sexually explicit jokes about women being told in the company of women and these were an affront to women. I attribute some of these negative reactions to cultural and gender differences too; men are not women and women are not men. Both sexes physically, mentally, socially and emotionally process things differently. It is not a negative. It is a reality. These differences led to uncomfortable positions in the work place that were real and needed to be resolved.

Sex discrimination was another legitimate problem in the work place. The knee jerk response was an over-zealous legal and political system ready to address these grievances and protect these poor victims. Some women became hypersensitive and others were simply and legitimately appalled by these situations. They needed justice for their long lists of work place grievances against men.

The legal system with the encouragement of the nanny state and the main stream media began to make laws against sex discrimination. The trial attorneys filed lawsuits; the media sensationalized the cases with the intention of correcting these injustices perpetrated by these men and corporations.

The federal government assisted in breaking the glass ceiling and piercing the corporate veil making companies liable for workplace sex discrimination. You can be sure that through government involvement and intervention some long lasting disaster was created. How many cases were bogus and how many were legitimate will never be known. You can find an attorney to represent a pile of dirt in this country for the right amount of money.

Those same ambulance chasing attorneys, many whom were women, then became politicians who created laws to pay damages to other attorneys; thus the legal circle of life. Let's just assume in the positive that the majority of legal cases and the government interference helped level the playing field and brought justice to the aggrieved. Call me a skeptic because I have serious doubts.

Yes, broken women were the oppressed victims who fought tooth and nail to be in the work place. They wanted to be secure in the work place on their terms and with no tolerance for others; that would be men. His sex or his terms were not relevant to the victim.

She could cry foul, start a lawsuit and men had no recourse to defend their position against the oppressed and physically inferior female victim. Think of the frivolous lawsuits or cases brought against Clarence Thomas, Bill O'Reilly or Bob Barker as examples of woman crying foul and playing the victim card. It is still a common occurrence in America.

All you have to do is turn on your TV, radio, or visit your favorite internet blog site to be bombarded with the pathetic state of women in America. Certain TV programs have huge female audiences that cater to the female victim and life changing moral issues that must be addressed. What shoes go with this purse?

Programs that endorses a woman's misperceived right to her reproductive organs, open sexual discussions about who is sleeping with who, or who is cheating on who's husbands, or who got married after their babies were born. These educational shows are provided by NPR, Oprah, Dr. Phil, Barbara Walters, the View, and numerous other progressively liberal programs. They are the staple of daytime TV and a good picture into the psyche of women in America. They encourage the behavior prior victims found so egregious in their quest for equality.

The pendulum has made a dramatic swing to the extreme left and it's taken a lot of American women with it. The Georgetown U student and Obama's female poster child, Sandra Fluke, is the perfect example of what is wrong with the type of American woman being puked upon American society today.

She attends school at one of America's top elite and most prestigious universities whose tuition is sky high (probably paid for by her parents or with government loans she'll never repay), bathed in the fountain of socialism and believes she is entitled to government provided contraception. She's is an excellent argument for keeping a woman barefoot and in the kitchen. We already pay for Fluke's contraception and have already been paying for it long before the travesty of Obamacare was passed and even before we read it. It's called abortion.

Not all women fit this victim mold. I personally appreciate all those conservative female icons who have suffered in the shadows of these liberal idiots. It's hard to balance being a super hero and victim at the same time. But damn those progressive women give it a good try and are equally, if not more responsible for the destruction of the extended and nuclear family than their male counterparts.

I was speaking with one of my sisters who told me how much she enjoyed Sex in the City (the TV show, not actually having sex in the city). I had a good laugh and she looked at me puzzled. My two older sisters were born in the 50s, came of age in the 70s, and are longtime proponents of women's rights and fighting for equality. They are currently reverting to their conservative roots because they realize the liberals are destroying the foundation of this country. It's been a very slow and tedious conversion. One is a lifelong public school teacher and the other lives I am sorry to say in the depraved socialist state of California. She is a writer for the degenerates in the entertainment industry; bless both their little hearts and may God help them!

In answer to my sister, I told her I don't understand why she so admires the characters in Sex and the City, the always and numerous liberal Desperate Housewives of every city in America, and most series on MTV, which promote women roles with all the characteristics that liberated women find so repulsive and offensive in men.

The premise of the shows are classic. They represent women behaving as men in high heels. Their primary concern is sex and physical satisfaction. I think every man can agree with this position (as we do with most positions!).

Cosmo is good with women having sex with multiple orgasms and multiple partners. The editors just don't think it is right for a man to have sex for him to have multiple orgasms and multiple partners. He is supposed to be monogamous otherwise he is a cheating dirt bag. You see sexism isn't just reserved for men. It is actively promoted by women also!

The next priority for today's woman in America is their job. Contemporary sitcoms rarely portray a mother at home. They all work outside the home and almost all are depicted as financially successful and don't need the money earned by a man. So far these women appear to behave just like men to me.

Men are revered for their strength and independence; so are women. Women self promote. They back stab their competition. They talk sex at the water cooler. They tell sexually explicit jokes in the office. They keep pictures on their desk (some that should be turned over). They are deceitful and cheat on their men, husbands or significant others in the workplace. Basically, they are exactly like men except for the victim thing.

Regrettably and all too frequently, the media present men as women or some gender bent twit. It is no wonder we are raising gender confused children and indoctrinating them in deviant behaviors portrayed as normal. This is another issue which we will discuss later.

In order to achieve what women perceive as equality, it became necessary to be what they were appalled by and fighting against. Some women in the work place are quite successful playing the traditional male roles. I am really impressed when they pull it off too! Women are indeed taking on the traditional roles of men and becoming mutant men which seems ironic considering their bra burning quest for independence from the tyranny and oppression of men.

The entertainment industry portrays women as hedonistic whores. I use the term as women have applied it to us men for years. I know you aren't allowed to call a victim a whore or any other derogatory sexist term. It is only acceptable for a victim to use the derogatory term when speaking of herself, some other woman or any man. One thing will never change. A man isn't going to crash and burn over being called a name like whore. He may punch you in the mouth but he won't be looking for an ambulance chaser to defend his manhood!

The entire entertainment industry, the major networks, cable and movie industry are not held accountable for anything. They portray women as sexually permissive and irresponsible. But if a conservative or a white man were to call a woman a negative remark the whole female hen house and every socialist sympathizer from coast to coast would start cackling and screeching from the top of the coops.

If the American woman thinks she is as intelligent and equal as she wants us to believe, how is it she doesn't realize that she is in actuality being manipulated by the government and the media? Since there isn't a valid argument for this observation, this is the perfect opportunity to present that victim card. It is one of those inconvenient truths we all have to face sometimes.

The growth from the oppressed woman of the 60's to their new role as faux male today, has been a bumpy and tumultuous road. Women could not only do the things that men could do, she was told she could do it all at one time and do it better than any man. Not just a man, but any man.

Women have been indoctrinated by the far left liberal establishment to believe and perpetuate these lies. In reality and truth, she is completely equal to her male counterpart and always has been. Neither a woman nor a man can do it all and do it all well. Equal is par, not superior. Inferior is a relative term to your mental capacity, not the value of your gender.

Our American sisters were misinformed socially and academically. She could try but she would fail because in reality no one, man nor woman, can do it all and succeed equally well at all tasks. It takes a team with each person playing their position. This is true at home and in the workplace.

If you try to do it all and be it all by yourself,
You will only succeed in doing it all half ass.

Who plays which role in the family is not as important as completing the responsibilities associated with each role. Accomplishing your tasks benefits you and your whole family. One person can only do so much. This is due to the limits and simplicity inherent of the human condition.

It is not that the traditional male role as the breadwinner was wrong. It is wrong when no one takes up the role of being the breadwinner and the government intercedes. It is not who is taking care of being responsible for the children; it is that no one is taking the responsibility for the children.

Both parents are failing as parents if they allow any government agency to take responsibility for their children or their family. Can you think of any case in this book where government hasn't actively moved to fill and control any voids? As the family unit is completely eliminated in America, America will cease to exist. You won't have to worry about equality; in its place will be complete tyranny.

The family begins from the point of dating, living together, marriage, and then raising children. You are building the relationship through stages and pairing up for life. During this union, the responsibilities increase and it becomes necessary to share those responsibilities. Whether the father stays at home or the mother stays at home is a decision between two adults and shouldn't be anyone else's business. It shouldn't be interfered with by government or inferred through subversive or subliminal TV programming. The results of trying to "do it all" by yourself, as a single mother or single father, provides a mediocre return at best; a complete failure at its worst.

A single parent could try to be father and mother, breadwinner, socially date, be active, raise the children alone, do the house work alone, cook the meals alone, and reach total nirvana all by themselves. In truth, they probably wouldn't do anything well, fail at much of it, often feel guilty, bruise their self-esteem and seek mental therapy in the process. This would happen if you were a man, woman or transgendered. We all have limits to our abilities even if we are physically different from each other.

Women are not victims now. They exercise their constitutional rights and make choices based on the options presented to them. They have total American guaranteed freedom to make those choices. The great minds and mentors of the drug induced Woodstock era lived and still live in a fog of euphoric false perceptions and are all too willing to subject us to their delusions. They are the ones who continue to promote the ideology of women being victims and yet the equivalent of men.

Their liberal ideologies put into practice have had a disastrous effect on the American family and the American woman. Women may think they have achieved equality, but at what costs to themselves and their family. The most the American woman can achieve or hope to achieve is sameness.

One reason that a lot of couples get divorced is because they couldn't do it all or someone wasn't doing their fair share in the relationship. You were tired, you lost interest in the relationship, you were unhappy and your spouse was unhappy. There were money problems. Did he cheat? Did you cheat? Cheating was probably a result of the failed relationship, not the cause for the failure of the relationship.

Are your children failing in school? Have you delegated your child development and progress to the public school system? Have you shirked your parental responsibilities because you just don't have the time? Do you work but live in poverty because you can't do it all by yourself? Have you become a spouse to the State? Have you passed your responsibilities on to the State? Are you on food stamps, welfare, Medicaid? Do you know who the child's father is? Are you taking responsibility for your own body?

If you have no responsibilities you have no purpose. If you have no purpose in the State's eyes, you then become expendable. Obamacare has a solution in regards to expendability. There are death panels in Obamacare that can and will deny medical care for those deemed useless to the state, provide no services or drain the system coffers. As a woman of no value to the state, will you be euthanized for the good of the state?

You can't use victimhood against the state. You can only use victimhood against your fellow Americans. The state promotes your victimhood for their benefit not yours. You are nothing but a useless pawn on a chess board of chaos.

What about the successful business woman? Often times they share roles with their husbands. But if they are both working, and both raising the kids, and both maintaining the house, they may chose to hire surrogates to fulfill some of the responsibilities. They may hire a housekeeper once a week or schedule a lawn care company. But they are tending to their primary family responsibilities and not relying on the state.

It's not unheard for a good parent to require their children work around the house and share some of the family responsibilities. The parents are still taking responsibility for their children and teaching them good work ethics. This in turn shows the children how to accept responsibility for one's actions. The entitlement mentality being engrained in our children's minds through public education today, the media and other socialist venues should cause great concern for the American mom and dad.

Entitlement indoctrination is exactly what is happening to our families when we pass our responsibilities on to the State? Any successful person, man or woman, single or married knows that you can't shrug off your responsibilities. You may have to turn to others in your community for assistance but there is nothing to be ashamed of in seeking help from others.

There is nothing wrong with needing help and reaching out to your family and local community. However, you should never transfer or relinquish your parental responsibilities to any government or religious institution. This is another reason why the liberal progressives have been so successful in destroying the American family unit.

We, and whatever dysfunctional family unit we have left, will become subservient and completely dependent on the state if we do not take responsibility for our family. Isn't it time to move on past the gender gap and extol the virtues and uniqueness of own gender?

When the government is successful in dividing us by class, race or gender, the government is all too ready to fill the gap. Isn't the victimhood argument a little dated and doesn't it play into the hand of the nanny state program. When you are independent, equal and successful, why would you need the government to interfere in your life? If women have achieved these goals why would you support the dissolution of the family unit in favor of a socialist state?

The American woman has achieved equal status with the American male; it wasn't that high a leap. She is no greater and no lesser than her male counterpart. Her uniqueness, individuality and role in the American family needs to be re-established and recognized for its importance to the family unit.

She is no longer socially or physically oppressed by her male companions in America, although crimes will always be committed against her for physical frailties.
Her strengths are maternal, compassionate, loving, and intelligent. Her emotions are sincere. She is physically and psychologically different than a man. But her differences are complimentary and necessary, providing the glue that secures the foundation of all families.

Those gender differences are important differences, but are in no way negative. They are a compliment to her human spirit. She is the perfect compliment in the man/woman relationship. Her strengths are uniquely feminine and should be acknowledged and embraced as such.

The American woman needs to protect and treasure her independence. Her worth to her family as wife, partner, mother, grandmother and matriarch is invaluable. Sons and daughters should cling to their mothers. That is the natural state of things; it is normal. The mother is the corner foundation of the family unit. Her role in the family needs to be secured, maintained and admired.

She doesn't need to be tied to a home or pigeon holed into a station in life. She is free to work, play and enjoy the benefits offered only in America. Do not let the liberal progressives and those organizations that encourage the use of the victim card be your guides in life.

If you are equal as I believe you to be, stand up for yourself and your family. I encourage you to nurture your relationships and remember how valuable you are as a friend, lover, wife and mother in America.

The liberal socialist cannot press forward with their regressive agenda without a willing victim. They need chaos to mask their agendas and true purpose. Women, on the other hand, have so much more to offer to their families, local communities and our country. You don't have to lower yourself to a position of perpetual victim anymore. You have achieved the sameness that your were seeking. The American woman needs to embrace her achievements, continue moving forward, and be at peace and comfortable in <u>her</u> valuable position in American society and the American family.

American Children

The greatest treasure of any country is their youth. They are the building blocks of the future. They are the ones to carry on the family name. They complete the family unit. The purpose of becoming husband and wife is to have children.

Good parents spend a good part of their lives first having and then raising their children. Good parents share their children's successes and failures. More importantly, these children are the future on which a nation will succeed or fail.

America is truly blessed with an abundance of natural resources. This nation is blessed with huge energy reserves, diverse eco systems and cultures. These resources combined with the ingenuity and drive of her people, has made America the envy of the world. America's children are above all, her greatest resource. Since America broke free from the yokes of European rule, she has taught her children the American work ethic.

The American dream insured that all American's could achieve success if they educated themselves and worked hard. The self made men like John Adams, Abraham Lincoln and Bill Gates, are honored and revered for their successes and achievements in America. This drive to succeed that led these men and many others like them to the pinnacle of personal and commercial success regrettably has been replaced with a debilitating attitude of entitlement.

America's children, our children, are now saddled with the disease of entitlement that robs them of any drive to excel. There is no drive because there is no necessity. They have been taught in colleges, government schools, by the 24/7 mass media, socialist politicians, and many selfish and inept parents, that they should expect to be taken care of by someone else.

They are not responsible for their positions in life. Someone else is responsible. Our children are complacent and have been taught that someone else is responsible for their needs. We are allowing an enormous disservice to be perpetrated on our youth in America.

In America today, more than 47 million people are on food stamps. The jury is still out on how many are truly in need or are just taking advantage of government largess. Don't ask, Don't tell started here at the doors of our US Treasury; not in the military.

Thousands of children are fed daily in school food programs provided by the government. In order not to stigmatize the parents or their children who receive food stamps and make the program seem morally acceptable to the masses, the government did away with the actual coupons and replaced them with debit cards. When you are at the grocery store checkout you can't tell if someone is on welfare because government debit card looks just like a normal bank debit card.

In order to gain total control over more Americans lives, the government has changed and lowered the necessary requirements to qualify for the disability slush fund too. A sad reality is that our government has no way to track the recipient, the purchases made or any related fraud that may occur in many of these entitlement programs.

No one is the wiser as to whom these people are who are mooching off the taxpayer. There is no shame for their children because that is all these children have ever known; all they have ever been taught at home and in school. Mom, Dad and Mom, or Dad have been milking the system and telling their children they were entitled to these unearned benefits.

This is a tragedy inflicted on the truly poor in our society and a gaping hole in the safety net that American's provided to really assist the poor. Therefore, the truly poor in need are ostracized by the majority of taxpayers who know the government is running a scam. They get lumped in with the majority of moochers who are not poor but who are scamming the system with the encouragement of the socialist in government.

I stated previously that these programs are the platform on which the Democrat party depends to stay in power and fundamentally transform America into a socialist third world country. Remember, we will feed you for free if you vote for us. These are the lessons our youth are learning in America; these are the lessons that have supplanted the independence and values of the extended family.

Our leaders keep enabling people not to work by increasing the amounts of time the unemployed people can keep receiving unemployment benefits. It has been proven that if you shorten the amount of time benefits will be paid, then the recipient will return sooner to gainful employment. Yes, they will miraculously find a job.

However, if you continue to pay these extended benefits, those same people will stay on the entitlement dole until they are forced off the program. The Democrats are never going to allow that to happen as long as they hold any political office and have unfettered access to the Treasury.

The main problem here is that our government is printing money it doesn't have and putting IOU's in the US Treasury (US Treasury Notes and Bills). These loans are to be paid back by future taxpayers; our children and grandchildren. The $17 trillion debt currently amassed by dishonest politicians, will saddle many more future generations in debt. This is the inheritance we are leaving to our children.

Social Security (which isn't an entitlement program, but an example of gov't mismanagement), and those on government unemployment take much more out than they have paid into the system. The Social Security fund would be solvent today if the funds paid into the system by working Americans hadn't been diverted by government to fund other entitlement programs. These are prime examples of why all federal entitlement and socially engineered programs are failures.

This is what we are teaching our children to expect that the government will bail you out. We, as American parents, are at fault as much if not more than the government. We have a propensity in America not to accept responsibility for our failures when things go wrong. It is always someone else's fault.

The government operates under the same premise. The President and Congress created and implemented these huge agencies, such as the Human Health Services, and then places any blame for the agency failures on the department they, the Congress or President, are responsible for overseeing.

This is why the President is responsible for a substantial number of illegal activities happening under his watch. You have the Fast and Furious Program (Dept of Justice), the dead Americans in Benghazi (Dept of State), the NSA spying on Americans (Executive Branch) and the IRS using their unprecedented powers to penalize and harass Conservative Americans (US Treasury Dept). You would think the President would have used the Department of Homeland Security instead of the U.S. Treasury to go after his political opponents. Maybe he did and it hasn't been uncovered yet. The point here is how those who govern don't take responsibility for their actions or inactions either.

We allowed the government to weasel its way into our family and have graciously relinquished many of our parental responsibilities to the detriment of our children. Now we seem to have relinquished all of our control and responsibilities for our family to the government. At least that is what the government would like you to believe. We allowed a lot of this circumvention and indoctrination to be implemented through the public education system while we were chasing the almighty dollar.

We have been blessed with abundant but not inexhaustible resources. After WWII, the American engine cranked up and we had big cars, big dreams and a currency backed by gold that had a finite value. Women entered the workforce and many homes now had two income earners. We had more money, but less time for our families and the children suffered. They still suffer, not necessarily materially, but emotionally and socially.

We didn't put off purchases until we could afford them, we began to abuse credit. The government dropped the gold standard and also began to abuse our credit. We practiced immediate gratification and that is what we passed on to our children. We taught our children that you are entitled to what you want when you want it. It is a shame we didn't teach them that first you have to work to achieve what you want.

While we were working, the government and media were teaching them they were entitled to receive whatever it is they needed or wanted. It is the right as an American citizen to have these expectations of entitlement. This is where we are in America. Our children have learned their lessons well.

Now of course, if America is going to continue to be the greatest country the planet has ever known, we are going to have to un-teach the entitlement lesson. If you look at the socialist countries of Greece, Spain, Portugal and the entire European Union, you will see that this is an impossible task.

I do not see any recourse to our pending implosion. It seems like America will have to collapse in on herself in order to rise again. We will have to rid our children of this pestilence of socialism and tyranny, removing all those who carry the "red" banners .There will most likely be bloodshed in the streets just like the last time America had to break the bonds of tyranny.

If we would add how these foreign countries are failing under socialism to our school curriculums, we could start to teach something of real value to our children. We may have to eliminate diversity training. But what the hell, we'll save a country in the process. We may have to re-instill the American work ethic and the value of earning what you need while saving to purchase what you want. These would be great lessons to teach our children,

It is up to each American, to reach out to their children. You need to talk to your children and explain what makes America such an outstanding nation. You have to instill the work ethic and the gratification one attains through the success of ones endeavors.

You DO have to stigmatize entitlements, noting that they should be sought as a last resort and a hand up instead of a hand out. You have to teach them that welfare programs are safety nets to help the less fortunate. They are not entitlements to be abused or used as a crutch.

Teach your children to admire others accomplishments and to strive for success themselves. Teach them not to be envious of others successes but to learn from them. You have to teach your children that the redistribution of wealth is an awful socialist and communist ideology. You have to teach your children that there will be greater and lesser persons than yourself and that we are NOT equal. We are different.

Teach your children that entitlements are an incurable cancer that eats away at wealth and savings of good hard working people while enabling bad people to be parasites and feed on what the government has confiscated and stolen.

In order to save America and the American family, you have to start with the children. You have to become parents again and take back all your responsibilities. You can't pick and choose which responsibilities. You have seen what happens when you relinquish anything to others or the government when it comes to your family. You need to provide your children a solid foundation and safe haven from which to grow. You need to protect your children from an over reaching and exceedingly evil government.

The sorry state of affairs that our country is in is because of failed socialist policies implemented by liberal progressives in the Democrat Party. It is intentional. Our country has been plagued the last 4 years and now the next 4 years with the worst possible occupant ever to sit in the Oval Office and a non-consequential Congress. This president intends to close the deal on our children by destroying the American economy and cementing their total dependence on the state.

President Obama has already issued numerous executive orders to bypass House of Representatives; the house of the people. You should be very afraid what his plans are for you and your children. He is not your friend. He is not looking out for your best interest. He harbors a deep animosity and resentment of the principles that America was founded on.

He is a proponent of socialism and wealth redistribution at the least, or a one world order progressive at worst. In any case, neither can be achieved without fundamentally changing America. Even if you think he gives a damn about you or your kids, you are mistaken. He has made it very clear what he wants for America. He wants to redistribute your wealth and give to each according to his need. This is socialism to the core.

He has professed to fundamentally change the country to his vision. It is a sure path to America's destruction and her loss of standing as a super power in the world. We do not have to follow or agree with his positions and we are within our American rights to voice dissent.

All of us owe our children a stable and solid foundation of love, faith, hope and charity. The extended family needs to be reconstructed to prominence in America. Then we can work on our local communities, then our states and with any luck, we can rebuild and revitalize this great nation from the bottom up!

The Reconstruction of the Extended Family-Conclusion

If America is going to succeed as a country of many diverse cultures, we have got to go back to her most valuable asset- the reconstruction of the Extended Family. It is a normal unit of procreation and order. It is the social foundation and very core from which a human is born and develops in this world. It is the grandparents, uncles, aunts, cousins, mothers, brothers, sisters and fathers that make up the extended family. We share this common bond with other primates and all animals in the animal kingdom. The pack, the flock, herd are animal communities. It is a normal and natural state.

I would be remiss at this juncture, if I didn't acknowledge an often hidden or overlooked member of our family. Historically they have been shunned by the world for religious or cultural reasons. Currently they are persecuted and killed in many countries around the world. However, America has developed an understanding and tolerance toward this deviant behavior.

American's do not necessarily condone, nor have we totally come to grips with this behavior, but America has made great strides in assimilating these persons into our culture. America is showing acceptance and tolerance on a very complex issue. That member of the family unit in American society is the homosexual.

They can be a father, mother, sister, brother, a cousin an aunt, uncle, grandfather or grandmother. America's core Christian foundation has always been intolerant of homosexuality. It is clearly stated in the Bible and other religious dogma that homosexuality is wrong and morally reprehensible.

I am not here to judge whether homosexuality is an offense to God. It is my belief that God will be the judge on judgment day and that all of us should live with our brothers and sisters in love, peace, compassion and understanding.

It is very difficult for all of us not to judge others. We are guilty of judging people every day. This exposes our true inadequacies and limits as human beings. There are a minority of gay people who are militants and degenerates, as with all people within our society. Even if they were victims of intolerance, the reciprocation of that intolerance does not promote their cause for acceptance and equality. Sex crimes are rampant on all sides of the spectrum and can't be limited to one "type" of people.

In America, the puritanical foundation of our culture considered all sex a private matter. This privacy spans many cultures in and outside of America. In my eyes that privacy is still a good thing should be practiced and respected more. It separates us from other animals in the animal kingdom. It also raises the importance of sex between two consenting adults to a truly personal experience.

Many people in America have sexual problems. They have dysfunction in the form of frigidity, erectile, premature ejaculation, STD's and a host of other issues. These are embarrassing situations for the individual. It seems appropriate that these issues and what goes on between two mature consenting adults should remain personal and private. These issues should also remain private between a patient and his/her doctor and not part of a government data base.

Imagine how difficult living "out of the closet" must be for the gay person in an intolerant society. In some countries today, you can still be stoned to death. Thankfully, America is not one of those countries. America's compassion and acceptance of all people is unparalleled in the world. Many of the colonies, which later became states, were founded by people seeking asylum, acceptance and peace in which to live their lives.

It is the foundation as penned by of our forefathers for an individual to be free in the pursuit of life, liberty and pursuit of happiness. This is the quest of all Americans regardless of color, creed or sexual orientation.

This does not mean we have to accept or participate in homosexuality or promote it as a societal norm. It is still a deviant behavior being it physiological or psychological is irrelevant. It just means we need to be tolerant of those different from us.

It is imperative that we understand that it is a biological anomaly and no one should be prejudiced for something they have no control over and that is inherent to their biological makeup. You certainly wouldn't discriminate against a physically handicapped or black person. In fact, we should not discriminate against anyone. There are plenty of laws on the books to discourage the injustices of discrimination.

If it is psychological, again would we discriminate against the mentally ill? America will have her issues and growing pains regarding homosexuality. But she is a complicated country sometimes reluctant, but always willing to grow and learn.

We don't need another victim class to help advance the socialist agenda. It bothers me that the same victim card that has been played for women, slaves whether black or red, is now being shuffled and added to the deck for homosexuals. We don't need another special class of Americans to divide us.

We need to stop this pendulum and quick. There has been considerable controversy regarding gay marriage. It appears to be basically an issue of semantics. Civil Unions/ Marriage are between a man and a woman. It carries different meanings to different people. One is the legal contract provided by the state (Civil Union). The other is a religious term sanctifying the bond between a man and a woman by the church (Marriage).

Civil Unions are contracts issued by the state authorizing the union between two people-normally a man and a woman. It has now been expanded in some states to mean the civil union between two people of any gender. It is the legal contract for the legitimacy of the American family and legal binding of two people. However, it is a legal state document and I think rightfully called a civil union, not a marriage.

The second definition is religious. It is the biblical marriage. A religious contract and is the bonding of man and woman as husband and wife before <u>God</u>. The laws of the church are not the laws of the land in America. The church and state are separate but each has its own laws, rules and regulations. This separation is practiced by all conservatives; the Democrat Party not so much.

Church law does dictate that marriage or the state of matrimony is between a man and a woman. This issue is a non-starter. Neither the church nor its members should be subject, or intruded on by the secular state. This protection is provided for in the US Constitution and not to be abridged. Therefore, I believe marriage should remain a bond between a man and a woman and their God.

I believe the state has an obligation to the homosexual community and atheists everywhere to provide legal means, legal contracts and foundations within common law to ensure that a bond or relationship between two people be available. Their assets, liabilities, benefits and debts, should be adjudicated efficiently through the legal system. It seems appropriate and proper that the legal contract between two adults issued by the state be called a Civil Union.

There is no need to ostracize the churches or their members who disagree that the definition of marriage needs to be expanded. Even though people claim conservatives are said to be intolerant, check out the intolerance of a liberal when you disagree with them and their entitlement programs. Look how hysterical liberal women become over abortion. They become totally unglued and you can always bet a sympathetic reporter is on the case with a world news headline on their behalf.

Secularists do not need civil unions to be called a marriage. They only need the legal contracts to legitimize their position. And although this does not adhere to my religious beliefs, I think civil unions are necessary to strengthen and advance the needs of the American family. I also believe that getting a divorce by anyone should be extremely difficult too!

Like all the other important members of the family, I would be more concerned with what the gay individual brought to the table and how they would tend to their responsibilities in the American family. They deserve no less than the rights guaranteed all Americans.

In our extended American family, we Americans will help care for the young and old. We will not depend on the government or other institutions to provide for our well being. We may need a hand up but we won't need a hand out. This is where and why our government has failed and continues to fail us today. But we were forewarned of the dangers of big government by those very statesmen who founded this great nation. We have been remiss and slack in our duties to protect America from the poisonous gas flowing out of Washington D.C.

You will always have people that need assistance whom have fallen outside the care and safety of the family unit. They will need a safety net and should seek one in their own communities. The government, especially a federal behemoth like ours, is the least likely and most inefficient organization to provide such humanitarian assistance.

 Americans have become too complacent and glutinous with our treasures. Our government has become bloated and self serving. It is crashing under its own weight and taking America people down with it. It has gotten so bad, that it is eating more than the American public can provide. It is building a debt that has not only consumed the current generation's earnings but is issuing IOU's on the backs of our children and grandchildren.

The days are coming soon when our federal government is going to implode or the entitlement class, the moochers, will rise in the streets trying to steal more from those who work and produce. One of these days those working people are going to say no to Uncle Sam and to the moochers. Then all hell is truly going to break loose.

When that time comes, and total chaos reigns, those who have traditional families will fare far better than those from the broken family that resides in the inner city plantation. The traditional families will bond with others in their communities and be prepared to defend themselves. It seems clear that the destruction of the extended family has been the single most effective way for government to gain control over the masses and take control of our country. We need to return to the extended family model. It may prove to be the most truly progressive idea yet.

More Yet to Come!

There are many more uncomfortable discussions to be explored and faced if we are ever going to get America back on the right track. We need to encourage the growth and welfare of the family unit. We need to take back our homes and work within our local communities to build a better America.

The States need to stand by their sovereignty and demand that the Federal government work within their limits of power enumerated in the US Constitution. We need to stop the forward movement of the Liberal Progressive Socialists that have infiltrated the Democrat Party.

We are a superpower because in many ways we are superior to other countries. We are a pure democratic republic founded by the people for the people. We do not have a dictator or king who rules by executive fiat, though to some it may appear that many in public office have definitely abused the privilege of serving the American people. We do not have two houses that are subservient to the Executive or Judicial branch. They are the houses of the people who should stand between the people and the tyranny of an overzealous and corrupted Executive and activist Judiciary.

There are two powers in the world. Good and Evil. No man can escape the grasp of either. The pendulum will continue to sway back and forth. Complete balance can never be achieved. But the good in man should always try and conquer the bad. At the very least, good should shine a light and expose the bad in bright light. This beacon of light will shine and always protect America as long as she seeks the Light.

Hopefully, I will be able to write more in the future. I have much to say and want my message true. I have no fear of progress, only what today's progressives espouse as progress. They truly are a regressive bunch of degenerates and they have reached the highest levels in our government, media and entertainment industry.

I embrace true progress because that is what America has always represented. She has been a country of progress, ingenuity and determination. She has protected her allies and defeated her foes. America is truly a great and exceptional country.

There are many foes within her borders I am afraid. Some are elected officials who hold very powerful positions. I wish they possessed Divine guidance instead of thinking they were the Divine. They have deceived the American people.

I fear only God or the possibility that my children and grandchildren will not be able to enjoy what has been up until now the greatest nation on earth. I have no fear of certain people or countries in the world that are jealous of our wealth or success. I have more fear of those who are enemies here in America that present themselves as our friends. A wolf in sheep's clothing, if you will.

I have faith in the American people and know they will wake up soon and notice something is terribly wrong. They will then realize those espousing the redistribution of wealth are the same thieves filling their pockets with our money and using the rest to buy votes. They provide no service of value, yet place themselves on tax payer provided golden thrones above the moochers they represent.

These politicians are the same hypocrites that hold office and these are the same foreign countries that suck out of the trough of our treasury. They bathe in the generosity given freely from our success as a nation. Foreign countries and many in our government feel we Americans have too much and our demise will mean their advance. The pendulum will swing again to the conservative right and the progressive left will be driven out of Washington and once again, relegated to the bowels of academia. God Bless America!!